"This book contains all the guidance most witches need for working with common magical herbs. Filled with useful ideas and applications."
Hearth Moon Rising, author of *Invoking Animal Magic*

"Rachel brings the magic of plants and herbs to life with her familiar, easy to follow style that is a delight to read. Her experience shines through in this volume that moves seamlessly from practical, common sense advice to matters of magic, meditation and spirit. This is a volume that not only is a joy to read cover to cover but should remain on any practicing witch's shelf as a constant point of reference. So often we forget the power of what seems mundane because it is familiar to us, and Rachel effortlessly recaptures the wonder of what we may see as weeds, and reminds us that we can strengthen our connection to the natural world through the magic and mystery of plants."
Mabh Savage, Celtic Witch and author of *A Modern Celt: Seeking the Ancestors.*

"Rachel Patterson's book A Kitchen Witch's Book of Magical Plants and Herbs is a wonderful resource for what can be a confusing subject. The author guides the reader through the intricacies of different aspects of plant magic, including astrological correspondences and working with plant spirits, with ease. Full of practical tips as well as metaphysical wisdom, and written with humour and an engaging style, this book is a must-have for anyone interested in the magical uses of plants."
Morgan Daimler, author of *Fairy Witchcraft* and *Where the Hawthorn Grows*

"I'm a herb and plant lover and have been all my life. Rachel's book is a delight, takes me back to learning with my family as well as forwards into new ways of working with herbs. There are lots of practical tips on growing and harvesting as well as star lore and the seasons as well as a very good list of herbs to use. Rachel advises *the* absolutely right way of learning from plants ... *"If you want to find out what magical property a particular herb or plant you have in front of you has, there is a very simple way...ask it!"* Rachel has it absolutely right, asking is the way. If you want to begin a love-affair with herbs this book is certainly for you."
Elen Sentier, *www.elensentier.co.uk*

A Kitchen Witch's World of Magical Plants & Herbs

A Kitchen Witch's World of Magical Plants & Herbs

Rachel Patterson

Winchester, UK
Washington, USA

First published by Moon Books, 2014
Moon Books is an imprint of John Hunt Publishing Ltd., Laurel House, Station Approach,
Alresford, Hants, SO24 9JH, UK
office1@jhpbooks.net
www.johnhuntpublishing.com
www.moon-books.net

For distributor details and how to order please visit the 'Ordering' section on our website.

ISBN: 978 1 78279 621 3

A CIP catalogue record for this book is available from the British Library.

Design: Stuart Davies
www.stuartdaviesart.com

Printed and bound by CPI Group (UK) Ltd, Croydon, CR0 4YY

We operate a distinctive and ethical publishing philosophy in all
areas of our business, from our global network of authors to
production and worldwide distribution.

CONTENTS

Who am I?

My craft name is Tansy Firedragon and I have been a witch for many years now. I have studied many areas of the Craft utilising books, online resources, schools and from studying with some wonderful mentors such as Janet Farrar and Gavin Bone. I have worked through the first, second and third Wiccan degrees.

A Kitchen Witch's World of Magical Plants & Herbs is my fifth published book with Moon Books. My earlier books are:

Pagan Portals: Kitchen Witchcraft

Grimoire of a Kitchen Witch

Pagan Portals: Hoodoo Folk Magic

Pagan Portals: Moon Magic

I am High Priestess of the Kitchen Witch coven where we run open rituals and Witchcraft and Goddess themed workshops.

I am an Elder at the online Kitchen Witch School of Natural Witchcraft.

My website: www.rachelpatterson.co.uk

My personal blog: www.tansyfiredragon.blogspot.co.uk

Email: tansyfiredragon@yahoo.com

Other websites:

www.kitchenwitchhearth.com

www.kitchenwitchhearth.wix.com/coven

www.goddesspathways.com

www.kitchenwitchuk.blogspot.co.uk

www.facebook.com/kitchenwitchuk

My craft is a combination of old religion Witchcraft, Wicca, Kitchen Witchery, Green Witchery and folk magic. My heart is that of a Kitchen Witch. I am blessed with a wonderful husband, lovely children, a fabulous family and good friends.

Introduction

Every plant, every flower, every herb and every tree has energy and that energy has magical properties.

This book is not about medicinal herb uses, but about magical ones, although you will find occasional tea recipes inside. The herbs, spices and plants I have included in this book are ones that are easily found or accessible whether it is by foraging in local hedgerows, growing in your garden, looking in your own cupboard / spice rack or purchasing from your local supermarket or garden centre (although I would suggest looking for a local Asian supermarket as they often have a huge selection of herbs and spices much cheaper than the supermarket). That's not to say the more unusual herbs and spices aren't powerful or magical, I just prefer to use whatever I have to hand, is easily found and kind to my pocket. At the end of the day the most important part when working with any ingredient in any spell work is *your* intent.

I have included some resins because incense blends work much better when they are included. Do some research, shop around; they can be purchased reasonably.

I work with herbs a lot in my magical practices, whether it's adding them to my cooking or my spell work. They are so versatile and a lot of them you have probably already got sitting in your cupboard or spice rack.

I add herbs to my candle magic spells, I make medicine pouches or mojo bags, I put them in witches' bottles, fill poppets with them, make magic powders with them, smudge my house with them, make incense with them and put them in my medicine bag. I also grow specific plants in my garden to attract the Fae and provide protection for my house.

All plants have spirits, and to connect with the magical property of each plant it is my suggestion that you talk to the spirit within it, make a connection. This is easily done, if you don't mind the neighbours thinking you are slightly mad. (More information on this can be found within the Plant Spirits and Energies chapter).

If you are able to grow herbs in your own garden, this is an excellent way of connecting with the magical energy as you follow the plant through its growth cycle. Don't worry if you can't, you can still connect with the energy of the herbs even if you buy them. I also collect all the petals from the flowers in my garden once they have 'gone over' and dry them. I also use some of the leaves and seed heads of the plants and dry them too.

Not only are they beautiful to look at and a source of nectar for the bees, flowers are incredibly special when it comes to magic. I think there are probably flowers of every single shade and colour – and again here you can use your colour magic to work with them. Blue flowers can be used to represent the element of water; purple ones would be good for psychic abilities and power, pink flowers for love and friendship, etc.

Of course each specific type of flower has its own magical meaning too. Flowers also have a language of their own dating back to Victorian times, when the flower that was given to you by a friend or intended had its very own message – forget-me-not would mean 'true love', daisy would mean 'innocence' and thistle would mean 'I will never forget thee', although I am not sure about some of the messages personally, such as sage which meant 'domestic virtues' and daffodil which meant 'delusive hope'.

There are also flowers associated with each month, which can be used in your magical workings. Whether you use the correspondence to tie in with the date you are working the spell or the month of birth for the person you are working the spell for, it will add power to it.

If you have purchased the herb or plant you are intending to use, hold it and try to connect with it; see if you can get a feel for its particular magical properties.

There are lists of magical correspondences in books and on the net and I will give you lots of ideas and examples within these pages too, but at the end of the day it is you who decides what works for your particular need. Just because someone else says one herb is good for prosperity doesn't mean it is necessarily the right one for you. If you really strongly feel that it is better for healing then go with your instinct.

You might work with a particular spell that asks for an ingredient you don't have or can't get hold of. In this case I suggest you come up with an alternative; go with what feels right for you. Run your hand slowly over your jars of herbs with the intent in mind and see what one 'feels' right; hopefully the best substitute will jump out at you. Although not literally, because that would be spooky... but who knows?

You will also need to charge each herb with your intent before using it. Take the amount of herb you need for your working and hold it in your hand or hold your hand over the pot it is in (only charge the amount you need, not the whole batch, as you may need to use the herb for another intent next time). Visualise your intent in your mind and then send that energy down through your hand and into the herb.

Plants not only have magical energies that lend themselves to spell working, such as prosperity, love and protection, they also have a gender. Some plants have female energies whilst others have male – useful to use when you need that sort of energy. Each plant will also be aligned to a certain planet and a certain element, again useful when you need that specific type of energy.

I have noted where particular herbs or plants are poisonous, but this book is all about magical plants *not* medicinal ones so, apart from the odd tea recipe, the contents of this book are for magical use only. This is your only warning – please make sure you identify the plants and herbs correctly. *Never* ingest any wild plant if you are not sure what it is or what it does. Don't apply essential oils straight onto skin if you are sensitive, always test a patch first. It is advisable to dilute all essentials oils with a carrier if you are going to use them on your skin.

Paracelsus (a Renaissance physician, botanist, alchemist and occultist) said: "Everything is poison; it is the dose that makes the medicine."

Growing, Harvesting and Storing Herbs

Growing Herbs

Herbs are generally easy plants to grow because they don't require a lot of care and space. They don't succumb easily to diseases or insect problems and will grow in most soil types.

Some important factors to consider when beginning an herb garden are that herbs need a good amount of sunlight – 4 to 6 hours a day preferably. They grow in most soil types except wet, badly drained soil. Although if you use pots then you can give them good soil and feed.

Even if you don't have a large garden (I live in the city so only have a small walled garden) you can grow herbs in pots. If you don't have a garden at all, hopefully you will have a spare windowsill or two that can house pots of herbs.

Harvesting and Storing Herbs

The best time to harvest an herb depends on the type of herb. Some need to be harvested just as the flower buds appear. The summer and autumn are the best times of the year.

Early morning is the best time of day to harvest herbs just after the sun has dried the leaves, but before it gets too hot.

Annual herbs can be harvested heavily, cut back just above a pair of leaves or a leaf, leaving 4-6 inches of stem. If it's the seeds you require, don't cut it back at all, leave it to flower and harvest once the seed heads are turning brown.

Perennial herbs should only have one third of the top growth harvested and sometimes just the tips of the leaves.

To harvest I use a pair of pruners or a sharp pair of scissors, but a sharp knife could be used as well.

Please… if you are picking herbs or flowers in the wild first of all make sure you have identified them properly (you do not want to poison yourself or cause a fatality!). Secondly, don't take the whole plant; make sure you leave enough so that it can continue to grow.

To dry bunches of herbs, wash them and allow them to dry, then tie the stems in a bundle and hang them upside down in a warm dark place (you can cover them in a brown bag). Leave them there for about 2-4 weeks. I use this method for herbs such as rosemary and bay; it works best with herbs that don't have high moisture content. For individual leaves or smaller herbs, lay them on a tray and keep it in a warm dark place. I use this method for rose petals or sometimes thyme with small stems. I find the best place is my conservatory as it gets very hot and herbs dry in no time at all, but be careful not to leave them in direct sunlight as it will fade their colour.

If you need herbs to be dried quicker, put them in an oven on a baking tray at around 180 degrees F for 3 to 4 hours. Or use the microwave, putting the clean herbs on a kitchen towel for 1 to 3 minutes, turning them over every 30 seconds.

Roots of some herbs can also be dried. Although some, such as liquorice, horseradish and marshmallow, work well if you peel the skin first, most roots like dandelion dry better with the skin left on – sometimes it is trial and error. Roots will also dry much better and more evenly with less likelihood of mould if you slice the roots into small pieces to dry.

To store dried herbs I prefer to use dark brown glass jars with airtight lids; keeping the light out extends the life of them. To freeze herbs, wash and blanch them, then drop them into ice water and place that in bags or ice cube trays to freeze. This works well with moisture-dense herbs such as basil, chives and parsley.

To make an herb vinegar, cover the herbs in white vinegar and steep for 4-6 weeks in bottles.

For herb butter, add 4 tablespoons of dried herbs and a squeeze of lemon juice to ½ lb of softened butter.

For herb mustard, mix 2 tablespoons dry mustard, the same

of salt and a teaspoon of sugar, blend to a paste with vinegar and mix with 1 tablespoon of herbs.

Herbs also work well in pot pourri – start with a base of rose petals and lavender then add whatever dried herbs you like, such as whole cloves or cinnamon. Add benzoin to fix, then store in an airtight jar for 4-5 weeks. Then it's ready.

You can also make flavoured sugar – add dried lavender heads or marjoram to a jar of sugar. It's wonderful to use in cookie or cake recipes. You can also use the stems of lavender on the fire to make your home smell nice.

If you intend to ingest any herbs or plants *please* make sure you have identified them properly first and also check dosage levels. If you are pregnant or breast feeding I would recommend not ingesting any of the herbs; it just isn't worth the risk.

Plant Spirits and Energies

Every single plant, tree, herb and flower will have its own very individual and unique energy. That energy can be used for magical or medicinal purposes. So you could use the herb, leaves, petals, root or seeds within your magical workings – magic powders, witches' bottles, mojo bags, etc. – or you could use the plant parts in medicinal teas, tinctures or salves. But you can also connect with the plant spirit and use its energies for healing, knowledge or seeking answers to questions.

If you want to find out what magical property a particular herb or plant you have in front of you has, there is a very simple way... ask it! Calm and centre yourself, have the plant or herb in front of you and slowly bring your hands up and towards the plant. As you do so, ask (out loud or in your mind) if you can connect with the plant's energy (its aura if you like). As your hands get closer to the plant you should start to feel a resistance coming from the 'bubble' that is the plant's energy field. As you connect with this energy ask what magical properties it holds; hopefully your intuition will answer you.

Plant spirit guides can also be connected with in various ways. Dreams and meditations are the easiest way to meet your plant ally. Before you go to sleep put out the intent that you would like to meet a plant spirit guide, in particular *your* plant spirit guide. You will often find that in your dream you will see a plant, tree or flower or you might smell the scent of an herb or even just hear the name of a plant mentioned in your dream. This will often be backed up by seeing that same plant the following day whilst out and about or on the television or in a book.

If you prefer to meditate, set out the intent that you want to meet your plant spirit guide before you make yourself comfortable, close your eyes and focus on your breathing, then see where your mind takes you and what landscape it leads you to.

Plant Spirit Guide Meditation

Make yourself comfortable in a quiet place where you won't be disturbed, if it is outside even better. Close your eyes and focus on your breathing... deep breaths in... deep breaths out...

As the world around you dissipates you find yourself beside an old grey and crumbling brick wall. You put your hand out and touch the cold stone. You start walking along beside the wall... You come to an old cast iron gate set into the stone. You gently push on the gate and it swings slowly open with a loud creak.

You pop your head around the gate to see what lies on the other side and are taken aback with the magical sight before you. Inside this old stone wall lies a beautiful garden.

There are rows and rows of gorgeous colourful flowers, lines and lines of vegetables all ready and waiting to be harvested and all surrounded by heavily laden fruit trees. You step inside...

Take a walk up and down the rows of flowers, make your way in between all the vegetable plots, smell each flower, taste the fruit from the trees, investigate the whole garden. Take in the sights, the scents and the sounds. Watch the bees and the butterflies as they flit from flower to flower.

As you are wandering around you come upon an old wooden bench so you sit and soak up the warm sun on your face and take in your whole surroundings.

As you sit... ask for your own personal plant guide to make itself known to you. You may get the name of a plant in your head or an image might appear... see what comes to you.

When the plant spirit guide makes itself known to you ask what it can do for you, what knowledge, guidance or healing it has to share...

When your plant spirit guide has finished communicating with you, give thanks for its time and guidance, know that it will always be available to you whenever you need it.

Then gradually make your way back out of the garden towards the gate in the wall. When you reach the gateway turn and take one last look back at the garden and know that you can return here anytime.

As you step through the gate you are brought back to the here and now.

Open your eyes and wriggle your fingers and toes.

Correspondences

I have included several correspondences for each herb, but these are generally either historical or my own personal ones – go with your *own* intuition when it comes to magical properties of plants. The energies will work better for you if you agree with the intent.

Along with the magical properties of each plant I have also included whether they align with female or male energies. This makes it useful when working with them, especially if you require them for God or Goddess work. Where possible I have included any links with horoscope signs; again this helps if you want to tie your herb magic into a specific horoscope phase or intent. And I have also noted down what planet the plant is aligned to if it has one; again this is all to help add weight and power to your magical workings.

Also listed are the elements that each plant corresponds to, yet more oomph added to your workings if the element aligns as well.

Here is a very basic guide:

Planet Characteristics

Moon: Emotions, intuition, divination, spirituality, cleansing, purity, unity, prosperity, psychic abilities, magic, change, feminine energy, the Goddess, personality, desires and cycles.

Mars: Passion, vitality, primal, aggression, motivation, strength, energy, sex, masculine energy, ambition, assertiveness, power, achievement, ROAR!

Mercury: Communication, confidence, acceptance, knowledge, adaptability, self expression, travel, skill and learning.

Jupiter: Influence, luck, prosperity, career, accomplishment, fulfilment, attainment, growth, opportunity, health and finances.

Venus: Love, lust, romance, fertility, money, healing, friendships, family, emotional attachments, hope, feminine energies, sharing, charm, grace.

Saturn: Renewal, changes, boundaries, restrictions, obstacles, protection, loss, blocking, holding, binding, the law, limitations, interruptions, returning and ambition.

Sun: Success, empowerment, ambition, enlightenment, goals, generosity, spirituality, male energies, health, vitality, the God, material wealth, pride, individuality and energy.

Horoscope Sign Characteristics

Aries (Mar 21ˢᵗ – Apr 20ᵗʰ): Ruled by Mars so it's a fiery ball of energy, encouragement, unstoppable, bold, hero action, caring, devoted, proud, impulsive, stubborn, reckless, leadership and jealous.

Taurus (Apr 21ˢᵗ – May 20ᵗʰ): Ruled by Venus so it is all about beauty and love, patience, organisation, support, romance, careful, dedication, stubborn, lazy, vain, over cautious, stability, over indulgent and a 'lil bit on the cheap side.

Gemini (May 21ˢᵗ – June 20ᵗʰ): Ruled by Mercury so let's talk communication, fascination, originality, adventure, versatile, wisdom, charm, resourceful, restless, distraction, judgement, depression, can get overwhelmed.

Cancer (June 21ˢᵗ – July 22ⁿᵈ): Ruled by the Moon so bring on the emotions, helpful, support, patience, compassion, romance, creativity, nurturing, gossip, isolation, overly sensitive, intuition, psychic abilities, lack of communication and can be a bit on the competitive side.

Leo (July 23ʳᵈ – Aug 22ⁿᵈ): Ruled by the Sun, bring it on! Courage, generosity, protection, loyalty, kindness, honest bare truth, entertainment, arrogant, jealous, power, optimism, aggressive and wasteful.

Virgo (Aug 23ʳᵈ – Sep 22ⁿᵈ): Another sign ruled by Mercury and communication, dedication, hardworking, practical, humour, resourceful, self destruction, uptight, critical and a tendency to have self pity parties.

Libra (Sep 23rd – Oct 22nd): More Venus with this one so bring on the lurve… charm, loveable, fairness, sincerity, sharing, romantic, vain, spoiled, delusions of grandeur, balance, harmony, manipulation, indecision and throw your arms up in the air drama queen (or king).

Scorpio (Oct 23rd – Nov 21st): Ruled by Pluto, full of power, rebirth, magnetism, passion, loyalty, protection, bravery, trendy, obsession, possession, organisation, transformation, jealousy, secrets, revenge, manipulation… ooh dark!

Sagittarius (Nov 22nd – Dec 21st): Feeling lucky coz this one is ruled by Jupiter, honesty, inspiration, optimism, fair, enthusiasm, encouraging, dedication, independence, education, arguments, recklessness, no tact, over confidence and a tad flaky.

Capricorn (Dec 22nd – Jan 19th): Ruled by Saturn, a planet of discipline (sit up straight) and maturity, loyalty, family, hard work, devotion, honesty, no fear, pessimism, no forgiveness, cold, materialistic, fairly hopeless and frankly sometimes a bit of a snob.

Aquarius (Jan 20th – Feb 18th): Ruled by Uranus so this one is a complete original! Communication, fair, logical, welcoming, an open mind, detachment, self destruction, irrational, desperation, guarded and a bit out of touch with reality on occasion.

Pisces (Feb 19th – Mar 20th): Ruled by the fantasy planet of Neptune, romance, wisdom, comfort, help, imagination, self pity, self destruction, gullible, a bit clingy and known to be occasionally on another planet completely – beam me up…

Element Characteristics

Earth: Stability, prosperity, money, home, strength, grounding, protection, nature, material matters, psychical, career, death and rebirth.

Air: Intellect, intuition, thought, mental power, communication, travel, divination, teaching, freedom, beginnings, creativity, psychic powers.

Fire: Passion, creativity, action, will, sex, anger, desire, energy, work, purification, destruction, strength, protection, healing.

Water: Emotions, love, dreams, compassion, psychic work, healing, cleansing, subconscious, purification, death and rebirth.

Crafts

Flower Fascinations

Fascination means 'to bewitch and hold spellbound', so flower fascinations are flower spells and charms.

If you put together the knowledge you have on magical properties within flowers, herbs and plants it is easy to make a flower fascination. It doesn't need to be fancy; just putting together corresponding flowers and herbs with the same intent into a vase will do the trick. Put the vase somewhere you will see it and visualise your intent each time you do.

Flower seeds can be added to medicine bags and charm bags then worn or kept with you.

Decorate a small besom or wreath with dried or fresh flowers with a particular intent in mind or to celebrate a sabbat or honour a specific deity.

Keeping a dried poppy head in your purse for prosperity, tying a bunch of sage over the front door for protection, putting herbs in a sachet to keep in the car for safety and protection – all of these are simple flower fascinations.

Flower Petal Beads

You can make beautiful beads from flower petals and even from leaves.

Gather together the petals and / or leaves from your chosen plant or plants and chop them up until they are really fine. Put the pieces in a food processor (or a blender) add a drop or two of water and pulse until you get a really fine texture; you may have to add more water, but do that a bit at a time so you don't make it overly soggy.

Put the mixture into a saucepan and simmer for about an hour. You may have to blend again after this until the mixture is really gooey and pasty.

Add a couple of drops of essential oil or food colouring at this stage if you would like to.

Then start forming the leafy / petal paste into bead shapes, small or large, but bear in mind they will shrink about 25% during the drying process. Then, using a needle, string the beads onto a thread.

Leave the thread of beads in a dry place and turn the beads daily so that they dry out evenly. You can charge the beads at this stage with your intent should you wish to do so. They will take 2 to 3 weeks to dry out properly.

Bookmarks

Herbal bookmarks are fairly simple to make and are lovely to use with your Book of Shadows.

Using pieces of cardboard cut a shape (oblong, square, oval, whatever you choose) to the size you require.

Place a design of pressed and dried flowers and leaves onto the cardboard. Lay it out first to see what it looks like and so that you can re-arrange it if necessary. When you are happy, glue each flower or leaf to the cardboard. Once your design is finished, you can cover the bookmark with sticky back plastic or pop it in the laminator. I like to finish it off by making a hole at the bottom of the bookmark (using one side of a hole punch) and then threading a piece of ribbon through.

Herb Candles

I have made candles from scratch before... and have ruined decent saucepans in the process and covered myself and the kitchen in wax, but if you like to make them with the melting and pouring method then adding herbs and flowers is easy. You can fix petals and leaves to the inside of your moulds before you pour the wax in or add a mixture of dried herbs as you pour. Each candle can be made for a specific intent by adding corresponding flowers or herbs.

However, if you like a much simpler version (as I do) you can dress an already made candle with essential oil and roll the candle in a mixture of crushed herbs, flowers or spices. If you are making something like a faerie wishes candle you could also add a bit of glitter to the mix too.

Circlets

I have several beautiful circlets that I wear in ritual; sometimes just on my hair and sometimes I pop the circlet over my top hat.

Mine are usually made from fake flowers, but always co-ordinated to the seasons – although in summer I occasionally wear one made from fresh ivy or any greenery stems from my garden. I find it easier to work with fake flowers to get them all tied together and to stay together when I move about!

If I am making a circlet from fake flowers I often start with a circle of wire first and then wind each flower stem or leaf onto the main circle, starting in one direction and continuing one stem at a time in the same direction. To finish I cover the circle with florist tape.

Incense

I make a lot of loose incense blends to burn on charcoal discs.

Start with a base, a resin is good such as frankincense or copal. Adding a wood of some sort helps your incense to burn longer too. Use something like sandalwood, or if you are using home grown dried herbs the woody stems of herbs can be added in too. Then the choice is up to you, whether you go for the scent you like or for the intent. Incense can be made for prosperity, love, success etc. but you can also make incense to correspond with the moon phase, a sabbat, a particular ritual or to honour a specific deity.

I also like to add a few drops of essential oil to my incense mix once I have finished it just to give it an extra boost of scent and power.

Remember as well that incense put together for magical purpose may not always smell particularly pleasant; it is the energies of the herbs that are important.

I would also suggest keeping it simple, too many ingredients and it gets complicated. Less is more as they say.

So pick your base resin and / or wood, tying them into your intent, and then add your herbs, spices and flowers – keep them corresponding to your intent. If you are making an incense to represent the element of air you would choose herbs that relate to that element, such as anise, lavender and mint perhaps. If you were making incense to honour the Goddess you might use lemon balm, geranium and thyme as these are all feminine herbs.

Don't forget that loose incense burnt on charcoal makes quite a bit of smoke!

Scented Paper

This makes lovely paper for your Book of Shadows or to use in spell work. Not only does it smell divine, but you can add specific intent to each page.

So simple... add a dab of your chosen essential oil to each corner of your sheet of paper and then allow it to dry – see I told you it was simple!

Scented Oils

You can make up your own essential oil blends quite easily, although it may take a bit of experimentation to get blends that smell just as you want them to.

Start with a base oil such as olive oil, almond oil or personally I like to use coconut oil. It is safer to dilute essential oils with a base oil if you are going to use them topically, especially if they are for use on children or the elderly. A 2% dilution is a safe guide, 1% for children. (Please consult a qualified aromatherapist if you are looking at using oils on children). I would not advise using essential oils if you are pregnant, some are safe, but personally I don't think it's worth taking the risk.

If I am creating a new blend I like to put a drop of each essential oil in a little bowl first to see if the scents work together before I make up a bottle.

For amounts, 30ml (1 fluid oz) of base oil works well with about 12 drops of essential oil.

You can also make your own scented oils from fresh herbs and petals. Take a base oil and add flower petals, herbs (just the leaves), spices (crushed) or citrus peel to the base oil, cover and leave to stand for 48 hours or so on a sunny windowsill giving the jar a shake every 12 hours. After 48 hours strain the liquid and throw away the herbs. If the oil does not have a strong enough scent repeat the process with fresh herbs / flowers / spices until you get the strength of scent that you want.

Flower Divination

You can make lovely pendulums with flower heads. Just tie one onto the end of a piece of thread and use it as you would with any pendulum.

Flowers can also be used to 'cast' in divination. You can do this using either a plain piece of cloth or a large bowl filled with water.

Gather together a selection of flower petals, heads and leaves. You will need to work out what flower part represents what, so a red rose petal might indicate love and a sage leaf might mean wishes, etc.

Once you have decided what each of your plant parts mean you can think of a question then cast the flowers onto your cloth or into the bowl of water. Where they land, what direction they land in, what other flower parts they land next to all will mean something – you will need to work out what.

Poppets

One of my personal favourite tools of the trade to use are

poppets, as they are versatile, easy to make and can be used for any intent. I like to make my poppets from coloured felt because I can work colour magic into each one and they are easy to sew. Each poppet can be filled with all sorts of herbs, flowers and spices with your particular intent.

Medicine Bags

This is another easy magical tool to make and again felt is easy to use, but if you prefer you can also use the readymade organza wedding favour bags that are easily available or if you have a few crafting skills you could work with fabric or leather. If you are using felt, leather or fabric cut out a circle (use a large glass to draw around) then charge each herb with your intent and pop it into the bag or onto the felt then tie it up with ribbon.

Natural Air Fresheners

You can make all sorts of scented and fragrant fresheners for your home and you can work magic into them by blending ingredients with a particular intent in mind, it might be peace, love, protection or just cleansing and purifying.

The easiest air freshener to make is pot pourri (yep, it's a bit 1970s but bear with me). It is basically very similar to a loose incense mix and I have even used herbal tea blends that I haven't liked the taste of but have loved the smell.

Use dried flowers, spices and herbs to make your blend. You can either pick ones that correspond with certain intents or just mix up the ones that you like the smell of. Magically charge each ingredient as you add it; if you want you can also add a few drops of essential oil then pop the mixture into a pretty bowl and leave it in your room. Pep up the scent occasionally with a few more drops of essential oil.

Scented Wax Discs

If you use oil burners as I do, you can also utilise them to melt scented wax discs. Just pop the wax disc in the top where you would usually put your essential oil. In fact, I always keep wax in the top as a base to add the oils to, then it doesn't burn.

You can make your own scented wax discs by melting candle wax (I use old ends and bits and pieces of left over candles – not spell ones though). When it is fully melted add essential oils or dried herbs of your choice then pour into silicone cup cake moulds and leave to set.

Carpet Fresh

To revive and freshen up carpets (especially if you have puppies, kittens or small children) you can use a base of baking soda to give the carpet a bit of pep.

Ingredients
6 tablespoons baking soda powder
1 tablespoon dried and powdered herb of your choice

Sprinkle on your carpet, leave for a few minutes, then vacuum up. If you have a particularly light / dark coloured carpet or a seriously expensive one please test a small patch in an inconspicuous area first.

Envelope Sachets

A very cheap and easy to make version of a medicine pouch, or just something pretty to make your room smell nice, is an envelope sachet.

Using an ordinary envelope or even a coloured one if you have it, make a symbolic or pretty design on the front using a pin to poke holes (a bit like dot to dot). If you are working a love spell you could make a heart design or if you work with runes you could pin-hole a rune symbol on the front. Go with what feels right for you and the intent of your working. If you are just making something to make the room smell nice then a flower design would work well.

Then fill the envelope with a dried herb mixture, again whatever works for you or corresponds to your magical intent. If you just want something that smells nice then use spices like clove and cinnamon; adding some dried orange peel would work well too.

Herbal Egg Decorations

This works really well for Ostara and the children can join in with decorating them. Use hard boiled eggs and keep the shell on or use egg shells that have had the raw insides blown out through a pin hole in the end. (The empty egg shells will obviously last longer than the hard boiled ones, but will be more fragile.)

Then, using a paintbrush, mark out a design on the egg shell with glue. Sprinkle or gently roll the egg in a layer of crushed herbs. Poppy seeds or ground seeds would also work well for this.

Herb and Pine Cone Fire Starters

For chemical-free fire starters these are brilliant. Take a sheet of newspaper and lay one or two small pinecones down the centre, then add a handful of dried herbs such as rosemary, sage or cinnamon sticks. Roll the newspaper up and tie the ends with twine. Place them in amongst the logs on your fire with the paper ends sticking out. To start the fire just set light to the ends of the newspaper.

If you are working magic then you could tie the intent of the herbs in with your magical workings – not only would your magical petitions be set into motion with the flames, but it will also get an added boost from the magical herbs in the fire too. In fact you could even write your wish / desire on a slip of paper and include it in the newspaper bundles so that it burns when the herbs and pine cones do.

Herbal Ice Lanterns

These are perfect for sabbat rituals using corresponding magical herbs.

Pour about 1½ inches of water into a 2-litre plastic soda bottle and freeze it (this forms the base).

When it has frozen put a slightly smaller plastic bottle inside leaving about a half inch gap all around, making sure it is central, then hold it in place with some masking tape. Place your herbs and greenery down the sides in between the two bottles. Bear in mind that if you use berries, seeds or spices they will float up to the top. Fill up the gap with water leaving about an inch and a half gap at the top to allow for the water to expand as it freezes.

When it is frozen fill the central bottle with hot water and gently, as the ice starts to melt a little, pull out the middle bottle. You can then either pour a little hot water over the outer bottle (be careful!) or cut away the plastic. This will leave you with your ice lantern. You can use a candle in the centre, but it will melt the ice much quicker so I recommend the battery powered candles.

Flower Essences

These are quite simple to make and work incredibly well. Decide what flower you want to use and ask the plant if you have permission to pick the flowers; you won't need many to make one small bottle of essence.

Pop the flowers into a bowl or jug and add spring water to cover them. Allow this to sit in direct sunshine for about 4 hours; this allows the energy from the flower to add its vibrations to the water. Then strain and pour the water into a bottle filling it up to half way (the small dark glass essential oil type bottles are best to use). Add the same amount of brandy to the water, so that you have equal amounts of water and brandy. Label the bottle with what flower essence it is and the date you made it, do the lid up and there you have it.

If you have leftover flower water you can drink it or pour it onto the ground as an offering. Add 2 or 3 drops of your flower essence to a glass of water and drink it to get the magical benefits of the flower.

Obviously, please don't use poisonous flowers!

Flower and Herb Wheels

Make a wreath using plants and herbs from your garden, tie them together with twine then write wishes on slips of paper.

This works well at rituals and gatherings where everyone can take part. Tuck the paper slips into the wreath. Once everyone has added their wishes you can put the wreath on a bonfire to burn it to release the magic.

Flower Mandalas

Mandalas are easy and fun to make and are so magical to work with. Use fallen petals and leaves from the plants in your garden or pick those that you need (after asking permission from the plant) and make a mandala pattern on your lawn or patio. As you add each petal or leaf make your request, adding your intent and positive energy into the pattern you are creating.

Smudge Sticks

Traditional smudge sticks are made using white sage, which is native to the USA and a different species to the sage we grow for culinary use. However, as I have tons of sage freely and freshly available in my garden, I use that instead of purchasing white sage. It seems to work perfectly well for me. I also like to add in lavender and rosemary when I make my smudge sticks. I find it easier to put together a small bundle of the herbs when they are fresh and tie them together with some string, then I let them partly dry. The herbs will shrink slightly, so then I re-tie them with new twine and allow them to dry fully. You have to make sure they are in a warm, dry place otherwise they will go mouldy. The alternative way is to allow the herbs to dry separately and then bind them together with twine once they are fully dry. To smudge a person, your home or sacred space, light the end of the smudge stick and let the flame die out so that the herbs are smouldering and making smoke. Waft the smoke around making sure it circles the whole person or every corner of your home.

Smudging can be done for various reasons. Using cedar works well to bring a calm atmosphere, juniper brings clarity and focus, pine is cleansing and strengthening, sage, lavender and rosemary all cleanse and banish negativity, while sweetgrass can be used to call in spirit. Be creative and see what works for you.

Psychic Herb Jar

Use this jar of magical herbs to increase and inspire your psychic, magical and mental powers. Add a variety of herbs to a clean jar. Give the jar a gentle shake, then inhale the scent before you do any psychic work.

You can add whatever herbs resonate with you for psychic purposes, but some good ones to use are cinnamon, cloves, sage, fennel, ginger, bay, borage, honeysuckle, marigold, mugwort, rose, mint, star anise, thyme and yarrow. You don't need to use all of these, just whichever ones feel right for you or add your own choices.

You could also make scent jars for other intents such as inspiration, concentration or meditation – pop the corresponding herbs in and take a whiff before you start drawing, painting, creating or meditating.

Magical Ink

Brilliant for writing in your Book of Shadows or for scribing petitions for spell work. You will need a nib pen or a sharpened quill / feather.

Use a clean jam jar and add crushed herbs – how many depends on how deep you want the colour, this is your chance to experiment. Then cover the herbs with vodka if you want to use a clear base or red wine if you want it a darker, fuller colour (you can use cheap wine, don't waste the good stuff!). Adding in black tea leaves or coffee will also deepen the colour. Leave your concoction to steep for around two weeks; test it half way to see how it is developing. You can also add food colouring if you wish. If you want your ink scented add in a splash or two of rose or lavender water. Dragon's blood resin makes a good ingredient, as do cinnamon and cloves, but play around and see what you come up with. Adding turmeric will give it a yellow / orange colour. When the liquid is ready strain out the bits and use the ink – keep it in the fridge and it will last longer.

Magic Powder

Sachet, magic, dusting or sprinkling powder (whatever you want to call it as essentially there are lots of names for the same thing) can be used to protect or purify your home or property. They can be used to sprinkle on your altar or candles to add intent or even to blow towards a person… the only limits here are your imagination. If you use a base of talcum powder and skin-safe herbs you can even use the powders on your body.

Start with a base such as sugar, corn flour (cornstarch), magnetic sand, salt, graveyard dirt or talcum powder then add your herbal ingredients to it. Go with your intuition about what herbs should be added and in what quantities, then grind all the ingredients in a pestle and mortar until they form a powder. If you don't have a pestle and mortar use the end of a rolling pin in a small dish.

These can be made for any intent so for a house protection blend you might use salt as a base because it is protective all by itself, then you could add rosemary and black pepper to it. For prosperity sachet powder you might start with a base of sugar (to make life sweet) then add basil and cinnamon. Go with the flow and experiment and see what blends and combinations work best for you.

Floating Candle Herb Jars

You can make these for any of the sabbats, to honour a specific deity or just to keep on your altar or table.

Use a clean jam jar or canning jar and fill it three quarters full with water then add in your choice of herbs; rosemary sprigs, berries, seeds, bay leaves, rose petals, etc. Work with the intent or just what looks pretty then float a tea light candle on the top.

Herb Paper Bowls

Create pretty bowls using paper and herbs, obviously these are just decorative and can't be used for food or liquids, but they make nice offering bowls.

Mix a paste with one part water to one part plain (all purpose) flour. Tear up pieces of paper and wet them in the paste then lay them onto a bowl placed upside down. Next lay flat herb leaves on the top, cover with a layer of torn up pieces of tissue paper (also dipped in the paste mix). Allow this to dry. The herbs should be visible through the top layer of tissue paper.

Plant and Herb List

African Violet (*Saintpaulia ionantha*)

You are probably familiar with this as a pot plant that we put indoors; they have dark green slightly hairy leaves and beautiful clusters of brightly coloured flowers.

Keep African violets in the house to increase and help maintain your spirituality (I think the dark purple flowering varieties are best for this). These little plants will also bring blessings and happiness to your home.

Although not its main magical function the African violet also brings a certain amount of protection with it.

African Violet Magical Properties

Protection, spirituality, blessings, happiness.

Ruling Planet: Venus
Element: Water
Gender: Feminine

Agrimony (*Agrimonia eupatoria or procera*)

A bright summer plant with tall spikes of yellow flowers, it also has sticky burrs and can be found in hedgerows, on roadsides and the edges of fields. Agrimony was used by the Anglo-Saxons as a healing plant. Harvest when the plant is in flower during the summer months; both the flowers and the leaves can be used.

It is used in Bach flower remedies to help people 'soldier on' and for people feeling out of balance.

One of the main magical uses for this herb is to reverse a spell or a hex and also to send it back to the person who cursed you in the first place. It is also very good to use in protection spells and to banish negative energy as well as being said to protect against goblins (I haven't tested this as I quite like goblins) and will help to hasten spiritual healing.

Add dried agrimony to a bucket of hot water when cleaning your floors to purify and bless your home. You can also add a couple of tablespoons of agrimony tea to your washing machine to cleanse negative energies from your clothes as you wash them.

Agrimony placed under your pillow is said to bring about a deep sleep and won't be broken until the herb is removed. This practice apparently dates back to medieval times. I would suggest that it actually makes a good sleeping pillow rather than bringing about a Sleeping Beauty incident.

Use dried agrimony in incense to clear the air, cleanse your aura and lighten your mood and also add it to witches' bottles around your house to bring luck and love to your home and family.

To Break a Hex Spell

Ingredients
A black candle
Slip of paper and pencil or pen
Pinch of dried agrimony
Cauldron or fire proof container

Light the candle and set it in a safe holder.

Write the name of the person who hexed you on the paper (if you know who it was) or you can write a chant, something along the lines of, "Whosoever sent the hex to me, return the favour, three times three." (OK so my poetry isn't so hot, but you get the gist). Then sprinkle some dried agrimony onto the paper and fold it up keeping the herbs inside. Then catch the paper alight from the candle and drop it into the cauldron to burn. Once the paper and herbs are ashes bury them. Blow the candle out and snap it in half; bury the candle parts with the ashes.

Happy Chappy Agrimony Tea

To boost happiness and balance your mood.

Ingredients
Either 6 fresh agrimony stems, leaves and flowers or 1 heaped
teaspoon dried agrimony
250ml/1 cup boiling water

Pour the water on the agrimony and infuse for 5-7 minutes,
strain and drink. You may want to sweeten the tea with a little
honey.

This tea blend can also be added to your bathwater to clear
negative energies.

Agrimony Magical Properties

Dispels negativity, reverses spells, aids spiritual healing,
cleanses the aura, brings sleep, happiness, luck, love, protection.

Ruling Planet: Jupiter
Sign: Cancer, Sagittarius
Element: Air
Gender: Masculine

Alexanders *(Smyrnium olusatrum)*

In Medieval Latin this plant was known as 'parsley of
Alexandria' *(Petroselinum Alexandrinum)* and was introduced to
Britain by the Romans. It likes to grow fairly close to the sea
although if you do find it inland it will usually be on chalky soil.

It is a biennial bush with leaves that appear at the end of
winter with fat round lime green flowers in the spring (you can
eat the buds).

It was often grown in monastery gardens as a vegetable and
for medicinal uses.

As for magical uses, to be honest I couldn't find any history or
research for its uses so the magical properties here are

completely my own.

As it likes to grow by the sea it works well in any kind of sea magic or workings that involve intuition or emotions.

It is medicinally said to be extremely good for clearing out your system, so it stands to reason to me that it works well in cleansing rituals and releasing workings.

Alexanders Magical Properties

Sea magic, intuition, emotions, cleansing, releasing.
Element: Water
Gender: Masculine

Aloe *(Aloe vera)*

This familiar house plant comes in all sorts of species. The leaves have spikes all along the edges and it likes to be in a warm place (a windowsill is perfect). The inside of the leaves are full of a sticky sap that is excellent for putting on burns.

In my house anyone mentioning aloe vera has to say it in a very funny deep Northern accent akin to "'Ello Vera"... no, I don't know why either.

With all the spikes it works as a good protective plant to keep in your home, but it also brings good luck and fortune.

Use the dried leaves in incense blends to work with the energy of the moon and any moon Goddesses.

Dab aloe vera juice on your third eye (middle of your forehead) to increase your psychic awareness.

The juice from this plant is very soothing so I think aloe vera works well to bring in calming energies too.

Aloe Magical Properties

Luck, protection, calming, moon magic, psychic abilities.
Ruling Planet: Moon, Saturn
Sign: Sagittarius
Element: Water

Gender: Feminine

Alyssum *(Alyssum spp. and Lobularia spp.)*

Usually grown as an annual this small plant has pretty white, red, yellow or purple flowers (depending on the variety) throughout the summer/early autumn.

Alyssum flowers encourage peace and can calm down arguments. Keep alyssum in your home to bring peace.

This plant brings protection with it, but especially against glamours.

Pop some dried alyssum in your bag or purse to keep your emotions balanced.

It is light and sweet and excellent for working with Goddess energies in her maiden form.

Alyssum flowers can also help you connect with your spirituality.

Alyssum Magical Properties

Protection, maiden magic, peace, calming, balance, spirituality.

Element: Air
Gender: Feminine

Anemone *(Anemone pulsatilla)*

A perennial spring flower plant with basal leaves and long leaf stems with single, pretty, brightly coloured flowers.

Anemone brings protection with it especially against negative energy. Use the flower petals in health and healing workings.

Anemone Magical Properties

Protection, healing, health.

Ruling Planet: Mars
Element: Fire
Gender: Masculine

Angelica *(Angelica archangelica)*

This is quite a tall plant that has hollow stems and small flowers in July followed by pale yellow fruit; it also has a large root. This is more familiar to me as the bright green sugary decorations that were used on trifles in the 1970s.

This plant has big protection powers; whether you grow it in your garden or use dried angelica in your workings it will bring protective energy in, keep negative energy out and bring in all sorts of protective angels and faeries (whatever your preference).

During the Dark Ages doctors dealing with the Black Death would place a piece of angelica root under their own tongues to protect them against the disease.

Sprinkle dried angelica around your property to bring prosperity in and burn as incense for blessings, purification and to aid with your divination powers.

Use dried angelica in healing workings. The root can be carried to bring good luck and inner courage.

Angelica root can be added to floor washes to purify and cleanse.

Mix dried angelica root with salt to use as an un-crossing powder.

Angelica Magical Properties

Protection, healing, exorcism, divination, prosperity, luck, hex breaking, courage.

Ruling Planet: Sun, Venus
Sign: Gemini, Cancer, Leo, Libra
Element: Fire
Gender: Masculine

Ash *(Fraxinus excelsior* or *F. americana)*

A beautiful tree with grey bark that turns into a scaly pattern as the tree ages and with pretty ash keys (the seeds) that hang from its branches, the ash is also in the same family as the olive tree.

The leaves appear in the spring and the black flower buds from the previous year grow into clusters of white or purple flowers. The seed keys arrive in the autumn.

The ash tree in Norse mythology is Yggdrasil, the World Tree or Tree of Life. Ash represents life and existence and that everything in the world is connected. The roots of the Tree of Life stretch down into the Underworld, the trunk is Earth and the branches stretch up into the realms of the Divine. It is often believed to be the tree that the Hanged Man dangles from on most Tarot cards.

Although ash is ruled by the sun and the element of fire, it is also linked to the moon and the element of water, bringing with it intuition and inspiration, showing once again the connection between all things.

Snakes are said to be repelled by ash leaves.

Ash leaves are good to tuck in corners and under mats in your home to bring protection and presumably to keep out those pesky snakes. To keep negative energy from entering your home place a piece of ash above your front door; also keeping a piece of ash on your altar will bring good health to you and your family. Carry a piece of ash with you when you travel on water to ensure a safe journey.

Wands made from ash are good to use when connecting with the spirit world or journeying to the Underworld and for healing. Place ash leaves under your pillow to encourage prophetic dreams. Carry ash leaves with you to lead you to attract a lover.

Besom handles are often made of ash. Ash is one of the triad of faery trees (with oak and hawthorn). If you want the Fae to leave you alone then you must stand in the shadow of an ash tree. To stop the faeries stealing your baby and exchanging it for a changeling you must put ash berries in the cot / crib (probably best to hang them above it or tie them under it rather than leave them rolling around in it).

Ash Magical Properties

Protection, prosperity, dispels negativity, improves health, sea magic, dreams, love, intuition.

Ruling Planet: Sun, Neptune
Element: Fire and Water
Gender: Masculine

Aster *(Callistephus chinensis)*

These are perennials with beautiful flowers that come in all sorts of colours and bloom between August and October.

A wash made from aster petals and leaves is excellent for cleansing and consecrating your altar and your magical tools.

Hang dried aster flowers in the highest part of your house (loft / attic if possible) to keep away negative energy.

The flowers carry a very definite feminine energy so are very good for working with the Goddess.

Use aster in incense blends to help you locate lost items.

Aster Magical Properties

Love, consecration, protection, Goddess, lost items.

Ruling Planet: Venus
Sign: Libra
Element: Water
Gender: Feminine

Basil *(Ocimum basilicum)*

Basil is a well known herb that I love to use in cooking and team with tomato and mozzarella in a salad. It is only an annual though, so won't survive outside during the winter. I keep a pot on my kitchen windowsill. The plant has soft tender stems with bright green shiny oval leaves that are highly scented. There are all sorts of different types of basil – Greek, lemon, Thai, purple, cinnamon and I have a very unusual smelling basil mint at the moment. One of the folk names for basil is 'witch's herb'.

Basilicum is from the Latin word basilisk, a snake-like creature that was said to cause madness and even death. Basil was eaten to ward against any such attack; so far I haven't been killed by a basilisk but I am not so sure about the madness...

It was said that witches used to drink basil juice before flying on their broomsticks; personally I would just add it to an incense blend to aid in astral projection!

Folklore states that basil seeds need be planted whilst hurling swear words about; this apparently dates back to the idea that swearing brought protection with it and caused any evil demons to be confused, allowing the plant to grow profusely.

Plant a pot of basil and look after it; when it is growing really well give it to someone you love. This will encourage love between you.

Pop a basil leaf in your purse to keep money coming in.

Rub a basil leaf on your skin to create a 'love attraction' perfume.

Write something that you wish to banish from your life on a basil leaf and leave it out in the sun to dry, then grind it up and burn it. As you burn it, it will release the negative energy.

Use basil in protection powders and exorcism and purification incense blends. It is also useful to pop in an incense blend to bring peace to a household after an argument.

Warning – be careful about over indulging on basil whilst pregnant.

Scorpio Incense Blend

Ingredients
1 part basil
1 part ivy
1 part copal
$1/_8{}^{th}$ part wormwood

Money Draw Magic Powder

Ingredients
One tablespoon sugar (brown sugar works best)
1 teaspoon dried basil
Sprinkle of ground cinnamon
Sprinkle of ground ginger

Grind all the ingredients together to a fine powder.

Basil Magical Properties:

Wealth, money, prosperity, love, exorcism, protection, happiness, peace.

Ruling Planet: Mars
Sign: Scorpio
Element: Fire
Gender: Masculine

Bay *(Laurus nobilis)*

The bay grows as a tree – the laurel – but it does grow slowly so it does very well in pots if you have a small garden. You can pick the bay leaves all year round.

Bay probably gets its association with psychic powers from being used in incense at the Delphic oracle.

Add bay to any spell work to give it a bit of a power boost.

Used dried bay leaves in incense blends to purify, cleanse, protect and bless your home and also to increase your spiritual and magical connections when in ritual.

Bay can also be used in pouches and powders to help increase your creativity and inspiration. Place a bay leaf under your pillow to bring insightful dreams. Write a wish on a bay leaf and bury it, burn it or send it off into the wind for it to come true.

Hang a bundle of bay leaves (or if you are feeling creative make a bay wreath) above your door to bring protection to your home. Also carry a bay leaf with you for personal protection and strength.

Bay Charm for Strength

Add bay leaves and marigold petals to a pouch and carry it with you to bring strength and energy; you could also use a yellow or orange pouch to add a bit of colour magic to it.

Bay Incense for Cleansing

Ingredients
Equal amounts of:
Bay leaf
Cinnamon stick
Rose petals

Pop in a small amount of myrrh or frankincense resin and mix together.

Bay Magical Properties.

Protection, purification, strength, power, healing, creativity, spirituality, psychic powers.

Ruling Planet: Sun
Sign: Aries, Leo
Element: Fire
Gender: Masculine

Beech *(Fagus sylvatica)*

There is a huge beech forest near where I live and they are beautiful trees especially in the autumn when the leaves turn a coppery colour. In spring the tree has small flowers and in autumn produces beech nuts.

Carry a piece of beech with you or burn as incense to increase your creativity. Use in sachets or pouches to make wishes upon.

Write your wish on a beech leaf or small piece of beech wood and burn or bury it to set the intent in motion.

Beech wood makes beautiful rune sets and good divining rods as it can help you see into the future. It also helps with your spirituality. A beech wand can be used to help open a channel to the Divine.

Carry beech with you for luck and success; particularly good if you pop some powdered beech into your right shoe (apparently).

The bark of the beech tree is excellent for carving and writing on, and good to use in spell work.

Preserved Beech Leaves

Lovely to use on your autumn altar.

Ingredients
450ml / just under 2 cups / ¾ pint glycerine
¾ litre / 3 ¾ cups / 1 ½ pints boiling water

This amount preserves about 10-12 sprigs of beech leaves. Cut away the lower small twigs and leaves so that you have a long stem. Crush the bottom couple of inches of the stem. Using a very large jug or container, pour the glycerine and hot water in. While the liquid is still hot stand the sprigs in the mixture. They will need to be left like that in a cool place for a couple of weeks. The undersides of the leaves will look a little oily; this means they are ready to lay on old newspaper on a flat surface for a couple of days. They can then be used in flower arrangements or decorations.

Beech Magical Properties

Wishes, creativity, spirituality, divination, luck, success.
Ruling Planet: Saturn
Sign: Sagittarius

Element: Air and Earth
Gender: Feminine

Belladonna *(Atropa belladonna)*

Belladonna or as I know it, deadly nightshade, is a perennial herbaceous plant. Warning: the whole plant is **EXTREMELY TOXIC** (the Romans used it as poison).

Whilst it has been used in spell work in the past for astral travel and in baneful magic I personally don't use it (way too much faffing to protect yourself). **ALWAYS** wear gloves when handling belladonna, always make sure if you use it in a medicine pouch it is securely wrapped so that nothing can get out – this plant is **DEADLY** poisonous.

Belladonna Magical Properties

Astral travel, baneful spells, crone magic.
Ruling Planet: Saturn, Mars
Element: Water
Gender: Feminine

Benzoin *(Styrax benzoin)*

This tree resin brings a calming and soothing energy with it that also increases your confidence.

As with most resins the smoke is good for purification and cleansing (anyone who has burnt resin on charcoal will know how much smoke it makes).

Use it in love magic for its zesty lust energy.

Burn it in incense blends for prosperity, especially in connection with your business.

Benzoin Magical Properties

Prosperity, purification, calming, confidence, love, lust.
Ruling Planet: Sun, Venus
Sign: Capricorn

Element: Air
Gender: Masculine

Bergamot *(Monarda didyma, Monarda fistulosa)*

This is a perennial garden herb with bright red flowers and large-toothed, pointed, oval leaves. The flowers grow at the top of long stems from midsummer onwards. There are also white and pink varieties. Bergamot is also a member of the mint family. Bees absolutely love bergamot; hence the folk name 'bee balm'. Use the leaves and flowers.

Bergamot in a sleep pillow ensures not only a sound sleep but also interesting dreams.

Rub a bergamot leaf in your hands and rub them together, this will encourage good friendships.

Keep a dried bergamot leaf in your wallet or purse to ensure money keeps coming in.

Sprinkle a powder made from ground bergamot around your home to ensure abundance and success.

Pop a pinch of dried bergamot into an incense blend to help develop your psychic abilities.

Bergamot Magical Properties

Abundance, meditation, sleep, dreams, clarity, friendship.

Sign: Gemini, Libra
Element: Air
Gender: Feminine

Bergamot (Orange) *(Mentha citrata)*

Quite different to the Monarda variety of bergamot, this one is a small tree that blossoms during the winter and produces fragrant yellow coloured fruits. This plant is used in Earl Grey tea and made into bergamot essential oil.

It is a good herb or scent to use in magical workings if you don't actually want to use a specific citrus fruit.

Carry orange bergamot leaves in your purse or wallet to bring money in or rub the leaves over money to make sure it keeps coming in.

It has the pure energy of the sun with it so use in any sun magical workings.

Mix with some frankincense and it makes a good banishing and purification blend.

Bergamot (Orange) Magical Properties

Money, uplifting, success, sun magic, banishing, purification.

Ruling Planet: Mercury, Sun
Sign: Virgo, Aquarius
Element: Air
Gender: Masculine

Betony (Wood) *(Stachys betonica, Betonica officinalis)*

Betony or as it is properly known, wood betony, is a pretty little wild plant but is packed full of uses especially medicinal ones. It grows in hedgerows, woodland clearings and on heaths. It has purple orchid-like flowers and quite unique toothed leaves. Pick the flowers before they open fully (use both the flowers and the leaves).

Definitely an herb of protection against evil, negative energy and, apparently, snakes. Growing betony in your garden will bring protection not only for your house but for all areas of your life. It was used throughout the Middle Ages for protection against witchcraft (but we don't need to go there). Carry betony with you for personal protection. Also a useful herb in amulets and sachets to help alleviate personal fears, to face our own shadows and bring relief for stress.

Carry it with you when you need to focus, concentrate or have a good memory such as for exams or tests or when you go up the stairs for something, get to the top and then can't remember what you went up there for.

Betony is also associated with the solar plexus so can aid in bringing about balance and harmony.

Place dried betony leaves under your pillow to keep away nightmares. Add dried betony flowers to your bath to ease depression and dispel fears. Add betony leaves to your witches' bottles to quell arguments.

Also an excellent herb to use in potions, incenses and sachet mixes if you are just feeling a bit 'hinky' and can't quite put your finger on the problem.

Take a Break – Wood Betony Medicine Pouch

Use a small organza pouch or a circle of felt and a piece of ribbon.

Fill it with dried betony, lavender buds and rose petals.

Carry it with you or place it under your pillow to bring about peace and stress relief; it will also help you sleep.

Betony Magical Properties

Love, purification, clarity, protection, anti intoxication, night-mares, anti depression, memory, stress relief.

Ruling Planet: Jupiter
Sign: Gemini, Sagittarius
Element: Fire
Gender: Masculine

Birch (*Betula pendula, Betula pubescens, Betula lenta, Betula alba*)

The birch tree can be spotted by its bright white bark and pretty light green leaves.

Birch is often used as the first tree for new colonisations so carries with it a huge amount of energy for new beginnings and changes.

Work with birch for new beginnings and the courage to release your fears.

Use birch twigs for purification and cleansing (historically birch twigs were used to beat out negative energy, but I don't think we need to go that far). Tie a bundle of birch twigs together with bright ribbon to sweep through your home to purify and cleanse and open the way for new beginnings.

Use birch twigs in fertility workings.

Keep birch with you for personal and psychic protection.

Birch makes excellent besoms and was often used to build cradles bringing protection for children.

Write your goals on birch strips or bark and visualise the realisation of your dreams. As you do so, burn the birch to set the intent.

Burn birch leaves in incense blends to help you attract love and to release that which no longer serves you.

Birch Magical Properties

Purification, protection, exorcism, new beginnings, courage, fertility, love, release.

Ruling Planet: Venus, Moon, Jupiter

Sign: Sagittarius

Element: Water, Air

Gender: Feminine

Black Pepper (*Piper nigrum*)

We probably all use black pepper on our food, but it has amazing magical properties too.

The black pepper corns we are familiar with are the berries (red in colour) that are picked before they are fully ripe from the pepper tree which can grow up to 20 feet tall. The seeds are then dried in the sun and turn black.

Black pepper corns are brilliant in protection sachets, bottles and amulets. They also help to release jealous thoughts and feelings.

This is also useful in powders to protect the boundaries of your property and to repel any negative energy. Mix ground black pepper corns with paprika and chilli powder to really bring in the protection.

Peppercorns also work well in personal amulets and pouches to bring out your inner strength and give you that hot peppery roar of confidence when you need it.

Used medicinally as a gargle, black pepper can paralyse the tongue so it makes sense to me to use the peppercorns in workings to stop people gossiping about you.

If you have a visitor at your house that you don't want to return, just after they have left you can throw a pinch of black pepper mixed with salt after them. This should prevent them from coming back.

Black Pepper Magical Properties

Protection, exorcism, jealousy, negativity, strength, confidence, gossip.

Ruling Planet: Mars
Element: Fire
Gender: Masculine

Blackthorn (Sloe) *(Prunus spinosa)*

A common spreading tree in hedgerows and woods, the fruit of which is the sloe (makes a nice gin…). Sloes can be picked throughout the autumn, but for magical use the leaves, twigs and thorns are what we want (be careful, the thorns are extremely sharp). Blackthorn also has pretty white blossoms in early spring.

Blackthorn is a useful wood to make divining rods from. Use it in protection and exorcism spells, pouches and incenses. The thorns particularly are good for protection and exorcism workings.

Folklore says that the blackthorn was a tree of bad magic and the wood was used by evil black magicians; I wonder if this stems from the viciously spiky thorns!

The wood is useful for healing as it has the power to cleanse and bring back good energy.

Walking Stick / Staff

Blackthorn branches make excellent walking sticks or staffs. Cut saplings when the trees are bare, trim off the side shoots, but not too close to the main stem. Leave it to season for about six months somewhere dry, such as a shed or garage. Then when it is seasoned trim the side shoots close and shape the handle by trimming with a knife and then smooth using sandpaper. You can use sandpaper to smooth over the whole stick if you wish and a polish with wood oil would help too.

Blackthorn Magic Ink

Crush a handful of sloes to release the juice, strain and et voila you have a very pretty red indelible ink to write magical petitions with.

Blackthorn Magical Properties

Protection, exorcism, divination, healing.

Ruling Planet: Saturn and Mars
Sign: Scorpio
Element: Fire
Gender: Masculine

Bladder wrack *(Fucus vesiculosus)*

Yep it's seaweed so you might need your wellies (or bare feet) to collect this one.

A brown coloured seaweed with little bubble air sacks found, unsurprisingly, on the seashore.

Carry a small piece of bladder wrack with you for protection on sea voyages, obviously dry it first otherwise it would be a bit slimy.

Use it in any kind of magic that requires the energy of the sea (don't forget to leave them an offering of thanks next time you visit the ocean). Bladder wrack also works well in weather magic especially when summoning up the winds.

Add dried bladder wrack to your floor wash to bring in more money; put a small piece under your doormat to bring money into the house too.

Add it to medicine pouches and sachet powders to help increase your psychic abilities.

Bladder Wrack Magical Properties
Protection, sea magic, money, psychic powers, weather magic.

Ruling Planet: Moon
Sign: Pisces
Element: Water
Gender: Feminine

Bleeding Heart *(Dicentra spectabilis, Dicentra formosa)*
You can find this in garden centres in the UK and it makes a nice perennial herbaceous border plant. The flowers hang like pendulums from the stalk in a row and are heart shaped.

The fact that the flowers are heart shaped makes them perfect for any kind of love magic.

Bleeding Heart Magical Properties
Love.

Ruling Planet: Venus
Element: Water
Gender: Feminine

Bluebell / Harebell *(Campanula rotundifolia, Hyacinthoides non-scripta)*
Two different species of plant, both with pretty blue bell-shaped flowers, that both seem to be called bluebell or harebell depending on what part of the world you are in. They also seem to have similar magical properties. Note: the Hyacinthoides

species is protected in the UK so please don't pick any in the wild.

The bluebell is definitely a flower of the faerie folk and also good for helping with shapeshifting magic. It is said to provide protection especially against witchcraft if you rub the flower on your body.

Use dried bluebells in magical workings to bring about the truth in a situation.

Add it to incense blends to aid with healing and to dispel illnesses.

Bluebell Magical Properties

Truth, shape shifting, protection, healing.

Ruling Planet: Mercury

Element: Water

Gender: Feminine

Borage *(Borago officinalis)*

Found in gardens for centuries, borage is a hardy annual with blue star-shaped flowers that appear from early summer right through until autumn and green leaves with a stem that is covered in white hairs. Left to its own devices it will self seed quite happily.

Increase your psychic abilities by drinking borage tea.

Keep borage flowers on the table when you do any kind of divination to help the reading.

Sprinkle borage around the house to bring in protection and use indoors to keep a peaceful household.

Roman soldiers would eat borage and medieval knights had the flower embroidered on scarves to bring them courage in battle – carry borage with you for courage and insight.

Use borage to bring about happiness (Pliny claimed that borage makes you happy) and to uplift your spirits.

It also works very well in a nice glass of chilled Pimms.

Borage Magical Properties

Psychic powers, courage, protection, happiness, peace.

Ruling Planet: Jupiter

Sign: Leo, Aquarius

Element: Air

Gender: Masculine

Bracken *(Pteridium spp)*

A large genus of coarse ferns with divided leaves, these are vascular plants that produce spores and small plants that produce sex cells (eggs and sperm). This plant is old... over 55 million years old; even its Latin name sounds like a dinosaur.

Because of its ability to produce sex cells it works very well in fertility spells.

Use it in all kinds of protection and healing workings.

Place bracken beneath your pillow to induce prophetic dreams.

Bracken Magical Properties

Healing, protection, fertility, dreams.

Ruling Planet: Mercury

Element: Air

Gender: Masculine

Broom *(Cytisus scoparius)*

This is a sturdy shrub with long green branches that are covered with yellow flowers in early summer, followed by seed pods.

If you can get hold of several branches of broom you can tie them together to make a symbolic broom to use for sweeping away negative energies in your home or around the circle in ritual. You can then use it for bringing in protection.

Broom can also be used for wind magic – either to calm the winds or whip one up.

The flowers are considered lucky and also protective if worn or carried.

Broom Magical Properties.

Purification, protection, luck, wind spell work.

Ruling Planet: Mars
Element: Air
Gender: Masculine

Burdock *(Arctium lappa)*

Burdock is a sturdy plant with a rosette of large leaves at the bottom with a tall stem that produces thistle-like red / purple flowers and burrs. Pick the leaves in the summer, the seeds in the autumn and the roots can be dug up in the spring or autumn.

As burdock is a hairy plant, folklore suggests that it will make your hair grow… there is no guarantee with this.

Burdock has many medicinal uses and has been used throughout history as such, so it stands to reason that it also works very well in any magical healing workings and spells; add it to your medicine pouches, witches' bottles and powders.

Keep dried burdock on you for personal protection. Grind burdock to a powder and use it to sprinkle around your home to create a protective boundary.

Burdock and Dandelion Wash

You will need about 25g of each root, chopped and added to 750ml of water in a pan. Simmer for about 20 minutes then strain. Add a couple of tablespoons of this burdock and dandelion wash to a bucket of hot water and use it to clean your floors. This will cleanse, purify and protect. It is also a good wash to use to cleanse your altar and tools.

Burdock Magical Properties

Protection, healing, cleansing.

Ruling Planet: Venus

Sign: Leo, Libra
Element: Water
Gender: Feminine

Buttercup *(Ranunculus bulbosus)*

I remember holding the innocent yellow flowers up to my chin when I was little to see if I liked butter. Obviously the answer was always yes.

Place buttercups on your altar as an offering to ask that your spiritual connection is strengthened. It can also help with divination and psychic abilities to see into the future.

Hang buttercups over your threshold to bring protection to your home.

Carry buttercup petals in your purse or wallet to bring abundance.

Buttercup Prosperity Pouch

Using an organza pouch or a piece of green felt and ribbon, add buttercup petals and a silver coin. If you are patient enough you could bind the petals to the silver coin with silver thread. Tie up the pouch and keep in your bag.

Buttercup Magical Properties

Abundance, ancient wisdom, divination, protection, psychic abilities.

Ruling Planet: Sun
Sign: Capricorn
Element: Fire
Gender: Masculine

Calamus *(Acorus calamus)*

Calamus is a perennial herb with tall green leaves not dissimilar to those of the iris. It also grows from a rhizome; the leaves and the rhizome are scented and have been used traditionally in scents and perfumes. Caution: some varieties of calamus are poisonous so please be very careful and make sure you have identified it correctly if you are intending to ingest it.

It grows near water so it does have watery moonlike energies, but the rhizome and leaves have a warm and spicy scent (along the lines of ginger, cinnamon and nutmeg) so it works well with Sun magic as well.

The story goes that Calamus was named after a man who fell in love with another man; unfortunately his lover died by drowning. Calamus spent so long beside the stream where his lover had drowned that the Gods turned him into a plant – with that myth in mind this herb works well in gay magic spells.

The leaves can also be used to weave together for ritual or magical purposes.

Sprinkle crushed calamus root around your property to keep out negative energy and provide protection.

Use calamus root in healing and health workings whether it is for physical, mental or spiritual healing.

Pop some calamus root in the corners of your house to keep money coming in.

Grow calamus in your garden to bring in protection, luck and abundance.

Calamus Magical Properties

Money, protection, healing, luck.

Ruling Planet: Moon, Sun
Element: Water
Gender: Feminine

Camellia *(Camellia japonica)*

This is *the* money flower and I just happen to have a very pretty pink one that grows in my garden, with dark evergreen glossy leaves and beautiful flowers (white, pinks, and reds).

Money, wealth, riches, abundance, luxury… do I need to go

on? It brings riches and opens your heart to the abundance of the universe... just don't forget to send a thank you note.

Keeping a camellia shrub growing in your garden should ensure that riches come your way and that you will never be short of money. Use the flower petals in money spells, pouches, poppets and witches' bottles.

Remember that wealth is not always in material form, camellia can bring spiritual riches too; just remember to be thankful for what you have.

I keep a few dried camellia petals in my money jar (the one I add all my loose change to).

Camellia Magical Properties

Abundance, prosperity, spirituality.

Ruling Planet: Moon
Element: Water
Gender: Feminine

Caraway *(Carum carvi)*

This is a biennial with large white flowers throughout June followed by the seeds (called fruits).

Keep a small pouch (secured safely) underneath a child's bed to keep them healthy.

Carry caraway seeds with you to increase your memory, attract love, ensure fidelity and bring you protection.

Sprinkle caraway seeds around your home to keep out unwanted guests.

Eat caraway seeds as a couple to ensure your love remains strong, spicy and true.

Caraway is a good spice to use during initiation rituals as it also brings with it the ability to increase your magical skills.

It is suggested that the faerie folk do not like caraway seeds so if you want to attract them you will need to hide these seeds out of the way.

Air Element Incense blend

Ingredients
Equal parts of each:
Benzoin resin
Caraway seeds
Lavender buds

Caraway Magical Properties
Lust, health, protection, memory, fidelity, love, initiation.
Ruling Planet: Mercury
Sign: Cancer, Gemini
Element: Air
Gender: Masculine

Cardamom *(Elettaria cardamomum)*
Cardamom is a lovely warm spice that not only brings heat to your food, but also to your passion. ...The seeds are the parts used and these are collected from the plant just before they ripen.

With the warmth of the spice it works well with lust and love spells, but is also stimulating to the body and mind, bringing clarity of thought and uplift to the spirit.

Add cardamom seeds to the food or drink you intend to share with a partner; it will add passion to your relationship.

Carry cardamom seeds with you to attract love. Add the pods to incense blends to use in your home to bring protection and love to the house.

Love Bath Blend
Pop these ingredients into a piece of muslin and tie it with ribbon then hang it under the tap as you run your bath to bring out a bit of va va voom...

Ingredients
3 sprigs rosemary
2 teaspoons lavender buds
3 cardamom pods

Ganesha Incense Blend

Ingredients
Half a cinnamon stick, crumbled
Three cardamom pods, cracked open
Half a teaspoon coriander seeds
One curry leaf.

Cardamom Magical Properties

Love, passion, clarity, uplifting, protection.
   Ruling Planet: Venus, Mars
   Element: Water
   Gender: Feminine

Carnation *(Dianthus caryophyllus)*

Carnations are probably one of the most common bunches of flowers purchased from supermarkets and petrol stations. They come in all sorts of colour variations and the cut flowers last for a long period of time in a vase of water. Carnation for me is *the* healing flower (it was used in the Middle Ages to ease fever).

Wear a carnation in your lapel to bring about personal courage; you could also add carnation petals to an amulet or charm. You all know the idea about going on a blind date and wearing a carnation in your button hole so that your date knows who you are? Well it also brings courage with it.

Hold a carnation flower in your hand and send any negative thoughts, emotions or feelings you have into the flower, let each petal soak it up then you can burn or bury it to take the negative energies away from you.

Carnation petals work especially well in healing spells, charms and pouches. Even just a vase of them placed next to the bed of a person who is unwell will work their magical healing.

Hang dried carnation buds over the threshold of your house to bring protection.

You can also work with colour magic using carnations; red for love, white for peace, yellow for happiness, etc. Go with what the colour of the flower says to you.

Carnation Tea for Strength and Healing

This is possibly the easiest tea in the whole world to make – all you need is 2 to 3 dried carnation flower heads. Pop them into a tea pot and pour on boiling water, steep for 3-5 minutes then drink to bring healing, good health and inner strength.

Healing Incense Blend

Ingredients
Equal parts of each:
Carnation flowers
Fennel seeds
Rosemary
Copal resin

Carnation Magical Properties

Healing, strength, protection, release, courage.
Ruling Planet: Sun
Element: Fire
Gender: Masculine

Catnip *(Nepeta cataria)*

Catnip is a member of the mint family, a perennial with leaves that cats seem to absolutely love the smell of. It produces small pale pink / white flowers throughout the summer.

To cats, this is *the* best thing, it's like the best drugs ever man... Sadly I don't own a cat... embarrassingly for a witch I am allergic to cats. I suspect it would work very well in an incense blend for Bast, but is good for any kind of cat magic.

It also works well in any spells for love, especially if you team it up with rose petals. Catnip is useful in fertility workings and to bring about courage.

Catnip also works well when added to incense blends to aid with shape shifting, astral travel and journeying.

Use the herb in dream pillows to bring about prophetic dreams. Keep the pillow away from your cat though, otherwise things could get messy.

Sprinkle dried catnip around your home to make your family and guests (and cats) feel happy and content.

If your cow has stopped giving milk and you suspect a witch's curse is the cause, use catnip with your spell to reverse it. Sheesh us witches get the blame for everything!

Catnip Magical Properties

Love, fertility, cat magic, dreams, happiness, courage.

Ruling Planet: Venus
Sign: Cancer, Libra
Element: Water
Gender: Feminine

Cedar *(Cedrus spp)*

A genus of conifer trees with spicy resinous strongly scented wood and evergreen needle leaves, cedar has barrel-shaped seed cones.

Amun-Ra's ceremonial barge was apparently made from cedar wood and King Solomon built his temple from cedar wood too. That makes it a good ingredient for any sun, male energy or God workings.

Cedar is a good wood to use for purification and protection, but is also good in money bringing charms.

The leaves of the cedar grow in spirals so this makes them excellent to use in any Goddess workings.

Cedar Magical Properties

Purification, money, protection, Goddess.

Ruling Planet: Sun, Jupiter
Sign: Sagittarius
Element: Fire
Gender: Masculine

Celandine *(Chelidonium majus)*

Celandine is a sprawling weed with dark green leaves and bright yellow flowers throughout the summer.

Use dried celandine leaves in amulets and pouches carried with you to help you escape from bad situations, abusive relationships or any limitations put upon you.

Carry celandine with you or use it in pouches to expedite legal matters and bring about a favourable result.

Keep dried celandine leaves in a witches' bottle or pouch on your altar to keep life happy and carefree.

Celandine Magical Properties

Happiness, protection, release, escape, legal matters.

Ruling Planet: Sun
Element: Fire
Gender: Masculine

Chamomile *(Chamaemelum nobile, Anthemis nobilis)*

Whenever I have had a long stressful day or I am in a bit of a grump my husband brings me chamomile tea in the hope that it will calm and appease me.

Chamomile does grow wild in some parts, but in Britain and the USA it is mostly cultivated. It is a low spreading lawn-like plant that has feathery leaves and small daisy-like flowers in late summer.

Grow chamomile in your garden to ensure that everything else there will be healthy and fertile.

Wash money (or perhaps just sprinkle the notes) with a chamomile wash (cold chamomile tea) to draw money to you or help you keep hold of it. You could also wash your hands in it as well. You could make your own tea, but I think it's actually easier to use chamomile tea bags. Keep a dried chamomile flower in your purse or wallet to bring in money.

Add a chamomile tea bag to your bath water to bring about love, peace and to cleanse and purify your body. Chamomile is also a good herb to add to your bath before any ritual work. Also use a chamomile tea bag in your floor wash water to cleanse negative energies from your home.

Use chamomile flowers in sleep pillows for a peaceful night and prophetic dreams and in incenses to purify.

It is good for cleansing and clearing the throat chakra and also for balancing all of your chakras.

Meditation Incense

Ingredients
Equal parts of each:
Chamomile
Sage
Vervain
Yarrow

Chamomile Magical Properties
Sleep, dreams, love, calm, money, relaxation, purification, balancing.
Ruling Planet: Sun
Sign: Leo

Element: Water
Gender: Masculine

Chestnut *(Castanea sativa)*

This is a large tree with dark grey bark that twists and furrows as the tree ages. It has large narrow pointed leaves that turn golden in the autumn. Catkins appear in the summer, which develop into shiny brown edible nuts that are encased in a spiky green husk.

Chestnuts are brilliant to use in any love workings.

Chestnut Magical Properties

Love.

Ruling Planet: Jupiter
Element: Fire
Gender: Masculine

Chickweed (Starwort) *(Stellaria media)*

A common weed that can be found all over the place, chickweed has pale green leaves, trailing with tiny white star-shaped flowers. It is loved by butterflies and insects to feed their larvae during the summer months so be careful when harvesting, try to pick the leaves and flowers in early summer and early autumn otherwise they may be full of little insect eggs!

At night the lower leaves of the chickweed plant fold up to protect the younger shoots so that makes it a good plant to use in protection spells for children.

Chickweed produces a lot of seeds, so this also makes the plant a useful one for fertility magic; add it to poppets and pouches.

Use the plant in sleep and dream pouches and pillows. A tea can also be made from it for the same purpose.

Carry chickweed or use it in pouches and poppets to attract love to you or, if you are in a relationship, to keep the fidelity strong.

Add a handful of chickweed in a piece of muslin to your bathwater before you go on a date to increase the chances of a love connection.

Chickweed Magical Properties

Love, fidelity, dreams, protection, fertility, moon magic.

Ruling Planet: Moon
Element: Water
Gender: Feminine

Chrysanthemum *(Chrysanthemum sinense)*

We are probably all familiar with the chrysanthemum and all the beautiful shapes and sizes that it comes in, with dark green leaves and flower heads full to bursting with petals. They flower towards the end of the summer.

Use dried chrysanthemum petals in spell work to keep things going, to make relationships, projects and situations last.

Keep the flowers in your home and garden to provide protection.

Use the flower heads to keep your connection to spirituality strong; keep them on your altar or pop them into a medicine pouch to carry with you. Carrying a chrysanthemum flower with you will also provide personal protection.

Eating chrysanthemum petals supposedly improves your mood.

Chrysanthemum flowers are often used in Samhain decorations or rituals.

Burn the flower heads (in a safe container) to smudge and bless your home.

The dried flower heads can be used to make a pleasant herbal tea.

Chrysanthemum Magical Properties

Longevity, spirituality, protection.

Ruling Planet: Sun
Element: Fire
Gender: Masculine

Cinnamon (*Cinnamomum zeylanicum, Cinnamomum verum*)

Such a fabulous scent and flavour packing a powerful punch of energy, cinnamon is made from the dried bark of the branches of the tree.

Burn cinnamon as incense to bring focus and concentration. This will also bring about a deeper spiritual connection and boost your psychic abilities.

Add cinnamon to sachets and pouches to bring about love and success. I often add a pinch of powdered cinnamon to any spell work that needs an extra boost of power. That cinnamon power punch also gives you the strength and courage to make necessary changes in your life.

Tie a bundle of cinnamon with a black or red ribbon and hang it in your hallway to bring protection, love and success to your household.

Wear a dab or two of cinnamon oil when you go on a date for added *ooh la la*. (Dilute it with a carrier oil first if your skin is sensitive).

Cinnamon Money Bowl

Ingredients
4 cups flour
1 cup salt
1 ½ cups hot water
1 tablespoon vegetable oil
Two teaspoons ground cinnamon

Make up salt dough by combining the salt, cinnamon and flour then add the water until the dough becomes elastic. Then add the oil and knead the dough (add more flour if the dough gets too sticky). Once it is a good consistency, form it into a bowl shape (it doesn't need to be perfect).

Bake it in the oven at 200C until hard (about 20-30 minutes); keep an eye on it so that it doesn't burn.

Place the bowl on your altar. When you need some fast cash take a piece of paper and write the amount of money that you need on it and place the paper in the cinnamon bowl and add one or two silver coins on top. Once the money you need comes in, burn or bury the paper and give the coins to charity. The bowl can be used again.

Other Uses for Salt Dough

You can use the same basic salt dough recipe to make any number of things; let your creative side run wild. You can also add in any herbs that you want to. I make salt dough offerings to leave when I am out and about in the woods using the recipe above (without the cinnamon) and cutting out small discs or star shapes. You can use the same dough to create Yule tree decorations and add in some glitter for a festive sparkle.

Cinnamon Magical Properties

Success, healing, power, psychic powers, protection, love, focus, lust, spirituality, changes.

Ruling Planet: Sun
Sign: Aries
Element: Fire
Gender: Masculine

Cinquefoil (Potentilla spp)

Usually an herbaceous perennial, cinquefoil can also be a shrub. The plants can be found growing all over the place really. Usually they have yellow flowers and the leaves are loved by caterpillars. The flowers and leaves are very similar in appearance to that of the strawberry plant.

Cinquefoil works very well in incense blends for divination and magic.

Add cinquefoil to pillows to help induce prophetic dreams and to sachets for love magic.

Hang cinquefoil above your doorway to bring in protection; it also works well in hex breaking spells.

The leaves have five points which represent love, money, health, power and wisdom.

In Hoodoo this plant is known as 'five finger grass'.

Cinquefoil Magical Properties
Protection, dreams, divination, magic, love, hex breaking.

Ruling Planet: Jupiter, Mercury

Sign: Taurus, Gemini

Element: Fire

Gender: Masculine

Cleavers (*Galium aparine*)
This is a sprawling annual, the leaves of which are set in whorls with small white flowers followed by small ball-shaped fruits. It is found in hedgerows, farmland and on river banks.

The roots of the cleavers plant can be used to make a red dye.

Lacemakers were known to stick the green seed of the cleavers to the heads of pins to stop them from sliding through the lace as they were making it.

I can remember playing with these as a child with friends, throwing them at each other so that they stuck to our clothes – and stick they do. These little plants are covered in tiny hooks that cleave to anything they touch, which is probably why they work so well in magical workings to do with commitment and keeping relationships together.

Add the dried plant to any of your workings where a situation needs bringing together, a relationship needs a bit of a hand or where commitment to something is needed.

Cleavers also work well in any kind of love workings and I would imagine they work well in binding spells... not that I would ever do such a thing of course.

Cleavers Magical Properties

Commitment, tenacity, relationships, love, binding.

Ruling Planet: Saturn
Element: Fire
Gender: Feminine

Clove *(Eugenia carophyllus, Syzygium aromaticum, Caryophyllus aromaticus)*

One of my favourite scents and flavours, cloves are grown on a small evergreen tree. They are the beginnings of the seeds that form just after the flowers.

Add cloves to incense to clear negative energy and increase the spiritual energy in your home.

Use clove oil as a love blessing or add a couple of drops to cider, mead or wine and share it with friends to bring your friendship closer. If you want to keep harmony amongst a group of people, charge a number of cloves with peace and friendship and then give one to each person to keep with them. If you want to attract a lover, cloves can be carried on you for that purpose too.

Keep a clove in your purse or wallet to attract abundance. I think the idea of cloves being for prosperity came about when they were an extremely expensive spice.

Hang a pouch of cloves above your door to stop gossip and bring about protection to those within your home.

Smelling the scent of cloves will ease tension and anxiety.

Truth Tea

Use this drink to help channel messages and bring about clarity and truth.

Ingredients
½ pint / 1 cup / 250ml of boiling water
½ cup honey
1 cinnamon stick
1 teaspoon vanilla extract
3 whole cloves

Pop the boiling water in a saucepan and add the other ingredients; stir until the honey dissolves. Then leave to cool. You can use it straight away, but it works better if you leave it for a few days.

You can also add alcohol to this if you want; add 1 pint / 2 cups / 500ml of rum to the cooled mixture.

Clove Magical Properties

Love, money, exorcism, clarity, protection, abundance, repels negativity, prevents gossip, stress relief, truth.
Ruling Planet: Jupiter
Sign: Aries
Element: Fire
Gender: Masculine

Clover *(Trifolium pratense, Trifolium repens)*

Clover is a common perennial plant with purple red or white flowers and small green leaves found growing on grassland and verges and flowering from late spring / early summer right through to autumn.

It is said to protect the virtuous against evil forces (well, that's me scuppered then…).

An old poem from 1815 by Sir Walter Scott states: "Trefoil,

vervain, St John's Wort, dill, hinder witches of their will." (Trefoil is clover).

We all know that four leaf clovers are lucky. The three leaves are believed to represent faith, hope and charity (love) and the fourth was God's grace.

Clover flowers can also be carried with you to bring luck and success your way.

White clover is useful in hex-breaking spell work.

Red clover works well for money, luck, love and exorcism workings.

Clover Magical Properties

Luck, money, protection, love, fidelity, exorcism, success.

Ruling Planet: Mercury

Sign: Aries

Element: Air

Gender: Masculine

Coltsfoot *(Tussilago farfara)*

Coltsfoot is a widespread plant that grows on damp waste ground, hedgerows and roadsides. Yellow flowers appear at the end of winter / early spring (similar to dandelions), growing on thick stems that have overlapping red scales. The flowers close at night. In late spring and summer large hoof-shaped leaves appear. The leaves also have a thick white felt on the underside and if you have the patience to collect some of it leave it out for the birds as they love to use it to line their nests.

Pick the leaves on a dry day with enough stalk so that you can hang them upside down in a warm dry room. They do take a while to dry, but when they are they can be crumbled and stored.

Burn coltsfoot in incense blends or use it in sachets and pouches for love and to bring visions along with positive energy to any of your workings. It also works well in incense blends to heal not only the physical but also the mental and spiritual too.

Use in workings to bring peace and tranquillity to yourself and your home.

Wear it in an amulet or sprinkle it around your home to attract new love to you. Coltsfoot can also be used in spell workings to bring a lover back to you.

Coltsfoot and Fennel Tea

Use two coltsfoot leaves in a pot and add a teaspoon of fennel seeds. Pour on hot water and allow it to steep for 5-7 minutes, strain and drink.

Coltsfoot Magical Properties

Visions, love, energy, health, tranquility, peace.

Ruling Planet: Venus
Sign: Taurus
Element: Water
Gender: Feminine

Columbine / Aquilegia (*Aquilegia canadensis, Aquilegia vulgaris*)

These are perennial plants found in fields and meadows. I have them in my garden and they self-seed everywhere. The Latin word for eagle is 'aquila', which reflects the shape of the flower petals as they resemble an eagle's claw. Columbine comes from the Latin word for 'dove' as the flower looks like five doves all sitting together (honestly it does... go have a look). Although the plant corresponds to the element of water I would also work with it as an air plant with the bird connection.

Use in all love magic as it has the power of Venus attached to it. This flower is also a favourite with the world of faerie.

Carry the flower with you to bring courage.

Add the flowers or seeds to your bathwater to help you gain clarity in a situation.

Use the leaves and flowers in any workings to dispel jealousy.

Columbine / Aquilegia Magical Properties:

Love, courage, faeries, clarity, jealousy.

Ruling Planet: Venus
Element: Water, Air
Gender: Feminine

Comfrey *(Symphytum officinale)*

A hairy fast growing plant with masses of green foliage and yellow or purple flowers, comfrey is often known by the folk names bone-knit or bone-set.

Comfrey has a long history of medicinal healing so is a perfect plant to use in magical pouches and powders for aiding in healing and bringing about good health.

It is good for using to bring something or some people together as it has powerful setting and 'knitting together' properties.

An excellent herb to use in travel pouches to ensure safe journeys.

Use comfrey root in money spells.

It is also very good to use in unhexing or uncrossing spell work.

Uncrossing Incense Blend

Ingredients
Equal parts of:
Comfrey
Elder
Basil
Bay

You can also use this blend in a muslin bag to drop into your bath water if you believe you have been cursed.

Comfrey Magical Properties

Money, travel, protection, healing, hex breaking, bringing together.

Ruling Planet: Saturn
Sign: Capricorn
Element: Water
Gender: Feminine

Copal *(Bursera odorata, Bursera fagaroides)*

Another tree resin, copal is a good base for incense blends. It is again very good for purification because of all the smoke it produces when burnt.

The sweet scent makes it useful for love workings, but it also brings protection with it.

Copal Magical Properties

Purification, love, protection.

Ruling Planet: Sun, Jupiter
Sign: Capricorn
Element: Fire
Gender: Masculine

Coriander *(Coriandrum sativum)*

An annual herb with bright green leaves growing on slim stems, coriander has pretty pale lilac flowers followed by tiny ball-shaped seeds that once dried have a lovely orange scent and taste. The leaves are one of the herbs that people either love or hate the taste of.

Coriander is mentioned on Babylonian clay tablets, was used by ancient Egyptians in the coffins of pharaohs for protection and in the *Arabian Nights* stories it was used as an aphrodisiac.

Use coriander to dispel negative energies and bring in protection, especially when working with astral travel.

Used for centuries as such, coriander is excellent in love

potions, sachets and amulets. Hang fresh coriander leaves above your threshold to bring peace and love into your home.

Wear coriander or carry it with you to attract love and also to help release the past.

Use it in health and healing workings of all kinds, as well as for prosperity.

Prosperity Incense Blend

Ingredients
Equal parts of each:
Coriander seeds
Cinnamon bark
Sandalwood chips

Coriander Magical Properties
Health, healing, peace, love, release, wealth, protection, negativity.

Ruling Planet: Mars
Sign: Aries
Element: Fire
Gender: Masculine

Cornflower / Batchelor's Buttons (*Centaurea cyanus*)
These pretty annual plants have ragged flowers that are usually in shades of blue, but they also come in pinks, reds and whites. I know them as cornflowers, but the name batchelor's buttons is also commonly used. The name cornflower may have come from their habit of growing in corn fields. It is endangered as a wild plant in the UK so if you see it out and about please don't pick it. The plant can be purchased from garden centres and grown in your own back garden for harvesting.

Keep it on your altar or use it in incense blends to enhance your psychic abilities.

Hang a pouch filled with cornflower petals in your cupboards to keep negative energy out and keep the flowers by your door to bring protection to your home.

Wear it as an amulet to attract a lover.

Because of its history growing in corn fields it is an excellent plant to use in fertility and abundance workings.

Cornflower can help us to see and work with the world of faerie.

Cornflower Ink

The petals make a lovely blue colour ink provided you use the blue variety of course.

Use a cup of cornflower petals and add them to two cups of boiling water in a saucepan; simmer until the water becomes a lovely blue colour (the volume of water should have reduced considerably by this time). Strain the liquid into a jar; add 3 drops of vinegar (this keeps the colour of the ink vibrant) and a pinch of salt (for preserving). Put a lid on the jar and give it a little shake. Store the ink out of direct sunlight.

Cornflower / Batchelor's Buttons Magical Properties

Love, psychic powers, protection, fertility, abundance, faeries.

Ruling Planet: Venus, Saturn

Element: Water, Earth

Gender: Feminine

Cowslip *(Primula veris)*

A very pretty spring plant, cowslip has yellow flowers that top a tall stalk.

Bring a pot of cowslip flowers into the house to bring peace and calm with it. Pop some dried cowslip flowers under your doormat to stop unwanted visitors from calling.

Carry dried cowslip to aid you in finding items that have been lost and to discover lost treasures, especially the immaterial ones.

Using a wash made from cowslip tea is said to keep you looking youthful (don't hold me to this one…).

Youth Tea

Add a couple of tablespoons to your bath or use as a face tonic to maintain youth (supposedly).

Ingredients
Two tablespoons of dried cowslip flowers
One sprig of rosemary

Pour on hot water and steep for 20 minutes, strain and then cool for a face wash or add to your bath water.

Cowslip Magical Properties

Healing, peace, calm, treasure, youth, anti-visitor.
Ruling Planet: Venus
Sign: Aries, Scorpio
Element: Water
Gender: Feminine

Cramp Bark (Guelder Rose) *(Viburnum opulus)*

This is a pretty small tree with white flower heads in summer and bright scarlet red berries in autumn. The leaves are green, but get a red tinge to them as the weather gets cooler. The berries are edible and the bark has lots of medicinal uses.

This plant says "take a chill pill". It can be used in incense blends and magical workings to bring about relaxation and allow you to let go of stress, anxiety and tension.

It has huge amounts of feminine energy so can also be used in any kind of girly magic (no… not that kind… well actually…) especially healing for those lady issues.

The berries can be used in Samhain rituals in place of blood and symbolise death and rebirth.

Use the dried berries to make a lovely red ink.

The berries and the bark can also be used in protection magic.

Cramp Bark Magical Properties

Relaxing, meditation, stress, tension, anxiety, healing, rebirth, protection.

Element: Earth

Gender: Feminine

Crocus *(Crocus vernus)*

Often one of the first signs that spring is on the way these pretty little flowers grow in woodlands, meadows and are cultivated in gardens. The crocus brings with it the promise of spring, new projects, new ideas and new ventures and, if you are looking for it, new love.

Grow crocus in your garden or bring a bowl of crocus indoors to promote love in your home. Keep a pot of crocus by your front door and they will bring happiness and hope to your house.

Visualise crocus or hold a crocus when you meditate and allow the spirit of the plant to take you on a journey and share its knowledge and wisdom with you via visions.

Crocus Magical Properties

Love, happiness, hope, visions, blessings, new beginnings.

Ruling Planet: Venus

Sign: Aquarius

Element: Water

Gender: Feminine

Cumin *(Cuminum cyminum)*

Cumin has blue / green leaves and white / pink flowers in the summer followed by huge dropping seed heads. It is very yummy in chilli recipes. Cumin was once used to pay taxes with… not sure that would work now though.

Spice up any love magic workings with the fiery lust of cumin.

Sprinkle items of value with cumin to prevent them from being stolen.

Place cumin under your bed to ensure fidelity, bear in mind that it does have a musky scent so you won't want to use a lot of it.

Wear it in an amulet to attract love and to bring about peace.

Sprinkle cumin around your property to bring in protection.

Add cumin to incense blends for abundance and success.

Cumin Magical Properties

Exorcism, protection, anti theft, fidelity, lust, peace, love, abundance, success.

Ruling Planet: Mars
Element: Fire
Gender: Masculine

Cyclamen *(Cyclamen spp)*

Growing in the cooler months, cyclamen comes in a variety of colours – red, pink and white, with pretty little flowers on the ends of stalks that rise up from a bed of ivy shaped leaves.

Keep cyclamen plants in the house to increase your self esteem, love and protection and to bring a general feeling of happiness.

Put cyclamen in your bedroom to help keep away nightmares and negative energies.

Cyclamen Magical Properties

Happiness, self esteem, protection, fertility, love, lust, nightmares.

Ruling Planet: Venus
Element: Water
Gender: Feminine

Cypress *(Cupressus sempervirens)*

This tree carries the joyful title of 'Tree of Death', but with that connection comes the magical energy of being able to help with easing grief at a time of loss. It also represents reincarnation.

Coffins were often made from cypress and the greenery was used in wreaths to represent eternal life.

Cypress is also useful to use in binding and releasing spell work along with protection and healing workings.

Hang a piece of cypress in your home to bring about protection and blessings to all who reside there.

Cypress wood makes a good healing wand; the cones of the cypress tree are also good in healing spells.

Cypress Magical Properties

Release, binding, grief, protection, healing.

Ruling Planet: Saturn

Sign: Aquarius

Element: Earth

Gender: Feminine

Daffodil *(Narcissus spp)*

Daffodils are one of my favourite flowers, such a welcome sight after the darkness of winter. Don't eat daffodils because that would be silly as they are poisonous.

Carry daffodil with you for all matters connected with the heart and keep them in the bedroom to increase fertility.

Daffodil brings with it the magic of rebirth so it is excellent to use in fertility workings.

Have daffodils growing in your garden to bring protection to your house and also to clear out negative energies. They are also good to use in workings to remove negative spells.

Having daffodils in the house brings luck, love and blessings to your home.

Daffodil Magical Properties

Luck, fertility, protection, love, exorcism.

Ruling Planet: Venus
Sign: Leo
Element: Water
Gender: Feminine

Daisy (*Chrysanthemum leucanthemum, Bellis perennis*)

Daisies make me think of summer, a big field of them and that makes me happy. Daisy is a perennial with green leaves and pretty white flowers that close up at night time.

"He loves me, he loves me not..." is an old folk rhyme that involves pulling off each of the petals one at a time chanting to find out whether he or she does indeed love you. This process can also bring you luck in love... not so much luck for the daisy though.

Hang them in children's bedrooms in a pouch (safely out of the way of tiny hands) to bring protection.

Have daisies in the house to make sure your home is filled with happiness, peace and joy.

Put dried daisy flowers under your pillow to bring about interesting dreams.

Use daisy flowers in love and lust pouches and spell work.

Because the daisy flower opens in the day light and loves to show its face to the sun it is full of solar energy, which can be harnessed and used in strength and courage spell work.

Daisy Magical Properties

Love, lust, protection, happiness, dreams, strength, courage.

Ruling Planet: Venus
Sign: Cancer, Taurus
Element: Water
Gender: Feminine

Dandelion *(Taraxacum officinale)*

We are probably all familiar with the dandelion, usually considered a weed but also incredibly useful for its medicinal properties and yummy as a salad leaf. Of course it has wonderful magical properties too. It is a perennial plant with a thick long tap root, long green leaves and bright yellow flowers that turn into fluffy seed heads.

Take a dandelion seed head and blow four times – once to each direction (north, east, south, west) – making a wish as you do so. I have also seen pretty little jars with dandelion seeds inside that are kept as wishing jars.

Use dandelion seeds in abundance in love spells and workings. The dried flower heads are also good in psychic power incense blends.

Making a tea from dandelion flowers is good to drink before any divination work.

Dandelion Divination Oil

Using a clean, dry jam jar, fill it with dandelion flowers then pour over extra virgin olive oil, making sure that there are no air pockets left. Then cover it with a piece of cloth and an elastic band (this allows any moisture to be released). Put the jar in a warm, sunny place such as a windowsill. You might need to poke the flowers under the oil level occasionally. About two weeks later the flowers should look limp and have lost most of their colour; strain the oil into a jug. Let the oil stand for a while so that any water from the flowers can sink to the bottom. Carefully pour the oil into bottles, leaving behind any water at the bottom of the jug.

This oil is actually very good as a muscle rub and for dry skin, but magically it can be used on your pulse points and temples before doing any divination to help increase your psychic connection. (You can also use it as a salad dressing!)

Dandelion Make A Wish Tea

Ingredients
Petals from one dandelion flower
1 teaspoon dried clover flowers
¼ teaspoon dried sage
1 cinnamon stick
1 teaspoon of honey

Put all the dry ingredients in a pot and add one cup of hot water, then steep for 5 minutes. Strain into a cup and add the honey. Stirring clockwise with the cinnamon stick, visualise your hopes, dreams and wishes coming true as you do so.

This mixture can also be used in wish pouches (without the honey and hot water obviously).

Dandelion Magical Properties
Wishes, divination, love, abundance, psychic powers.
Ruling Planet: Jupiter
Sign: Taurus
Element: Air
Gender: Masculine

Datura *(Datura stramonium)*
The datura or 'moonflower' is a leafy annual or short lived perennial that likes it warm; in the UK it is best grown in conservatories. It has trumpet shaped flowers that are followed by spiny seed pods. Caution: this plant is **TOXIC**.

This plant has a very strong kick-bottom type of feminine energy and when used in love workings it takes no prisoners... you have been warned.

It does work well in protection and hex breaking spell work, but also in dream work – you **DO NOT** have to eat it, just use it in medicine pouches.

Datura Magical Properties

Protection, feminine energy, hex breaking, dreams.

Ruling Planet: Saturn, Venus
Element: Water
Gender: Feminine

Delphinium / Larkspur *(Delphinium spp)*

Delphiniums are perennial flowering plants often referred to as larkspur. Plants within the genus range from alpine plants to shrubs. Flowers bloom from late spring to late summer and come in a range of colours: white, pink, blue, purple, yellow and red. Caution: don't eat it, the plant is poisonous.

Delphinium is an excellent protective herb said to be good for keeping warriors safe and also protects against snakes, scorpions and ghosts, possibly not all at once.

It is also a lovely flower to use in midsummer celebrations and will attract the Fae.

One myth tells of the delphinium flowers being created by drops of dragon blood, so this would work well in dragon magic too.

Delphinium Magical Properties

Protection, midsummer, faeries, dragons.

Ruling Planet: Venus
Element: Water
Gender: Feminine

Dill *(Anethum graveolens)*

This is a hardy annual herb that has lacy feathery leaves with yellow flowers on tall stems.

Dill seeds can be placed around your home to bring in protection. They also work well in anti-jealousy spell work.

Use the flowers in love sachets, pouches and spell work.

Keep dill seeds in your purse or wallet or grow the plant in your garden to bring in money.

Add a sprinkling of dill seeds to your bath water before you go on a date to make you irresistible... don't hold me responsible for the consequences.

Carry dill with you to bring about balance between your conscious and unconscious. It can also bring clarity and insight.

Burn in incense blends to help bring knowledge and wisdom and it will also help with your magical powers.

It was given to witches to help break their willpower... I may avoid this one as I don't have any will power to start with.

Dill Magical Properties

Protection, love, lust, money, jealousy, balance, clarity, knowledge, magic.

Ruling Planet: Mercury
Sign: Cancer, Gemini, Leo
Element: Fire
Gender: Masculine

Dittany

There are two main dittany plants:

Origanum dictamnus

Dittany of Crete, this is a tender perennial plant used for healing that only grows on the mountains of Crete. It is on the list of threatened plant species.

Historically, this is a powerful herb to use in love magic.

Use in incense blends to help you connect with spirit and aid with prophetic visions.

Sprinkle around you home for protection.

Dittany of Crete Magical Properties

Love, spirit work, visions, protection.

Ruling Planet: Venus

Element: Water
Gender: Feminine

Dictamnus albus

This is a pretty herbaceous perennial also known as 'false dittany' or 'burning bush'. Its flowers are on tall spikes ranging from white to pale purple. During the summer the plant is covered with a flammable substance that gives off a gas. If it catches fire it looks as if the plant is indeed burning.

Use dittany *(Dictamnus albus)* for fire element workings and in Samhain rituals.

Dittany Magical Properties

Fire, Samhain.
Ruling Planet: Moon
Element: Fire
Gender: Feminine

Dock *(Rumex spp., R. crispus, R. obtusifolius)*

I remember using dock leaves as a child to take the sting away after being stung by stinging nettles.

Dock has large tough dark green leaves that have wavy edges, clusters of green flowers that turn red as they get older followed by seeds in the autumn.

Use dock seeds for cleansing and purifying and also for fertility.

Sprinkle dock seeds around your house or use them in incense blends to bring in abundance and protection. Do the same for your business to attract new custom.

Wear dock in an amulet to bring new love or fertility to you.

Dock Magical Properties

Money, healing, fertility, cleansing, love, purification.
Ruling Planet: Jupiter

Element: Air
Gender: Masculine

Dogwood *(Cornus florida)*

This is a deciduous tree with white flowers in spring followed by oval berries.

It is dogwood, so if you need the energy of dog animal magic then this is your plant to work with, everything that a dog is: loyal, trustworthy, faithful and protective, only this won't leave hairs on the couch.

Dogwood Magical Properties

Loyalty, trust, faithful, protective.
Element: Earth
Gender: Masculine

Dragon's Blood *(Daemonorops draco, Daemonorops propinquos)*

This is a tree resin that comes commonly from the *Daemonorops* genus of trees although it also comes from the *Dracaena* species. You may find that some medieval texts claim it comes from real dragons that died in mortal combat...

If I feel a magical working needs an extra boost of power I add in a pinch of ground dragon's blood to give it an extra kick.

It also brings the mighty power of the dragon with it for use in protection incense blends and spell work and of course any fire elemental workings as well.

Pop a piece of dragon's blood resin under your pillow to bring love into your life.

Add it to incense blends to attract love, happiness and joy to your home.

Even though you are using the 'blood' of a dragon, he won't mind if you use it for dragon magic.

Dragon's Blood Magical Properties

Power, protection, love, happiness, dragon magic.

Ruling Planet: Mars
Sign: Aries
Element: Fire
Gender: Masculine

Dulse *(Palmaria palmata)*

It's seaweed time... a red seaweed found... on seashores (yep, bet you were surprised about that one). Pick it during June and September. It is apparently quite tasty, but don't forget to wash off the snails and shells first.

To dry seaweed, rinse it in clean water to remove any sand (and those snails) then lay it on newspaper or muslin preferably outside in the sunshine to dry until crisp, then it can be stored in jars.

Sprinkle dried ground dulse on your meal and that of your loved one to increase your desire for each other.

Hang a piece of dulse (dried, not still wet and soggy) over your front door to bring protection for your home.

Use dried dulse in your home to bring in harmony, love and peace.

Dulse Magical Properties

Lust, love, harmony, peace, protection.

Ruling Planet: Moon
Sign: Pisces
Element: Water
Gender: Feminine

Echinacea *(Echinacea spp)*

These herbaceous perennial plants are grown from tap roots with colourful flowers on long stems often called 'coneflowers'.

Echinacea lends itself very well to any kind of crone magic.

Medicinally it is used to boost the immune system so it works well in healing spells.

Add a sprinkle of echinacea to other workings to increase their power.

Keep some dried petals in your purse or wallet to attract abundance.

Echinacea Magical Properties

Crone magic, power, healing, abundance.

Ruling Planet: Venus, Mars

Element: Earth

Gender: Feminine

Elder *(Sambucus nigra / canadensis)*

Elder is a small deciduous tree (or shrub) that grows in woods, hedgerows and on waste ground. The trunk is quite often crooked and low lying with rugged bark. It has dark green leaves that have quite an unpleasant smell, but the flowers that appear in early summer are pretty and fragrant with large flat bunches of white flowers. They ripen into berries that are green at first and then a dark purple colour by early autumn.

Described in the past as a 'whole medicine chest' in one tree, the elder is an excellent ingredient to use in healing spell work.

The stem was said to have been used by Prometheus to bring fire to man from the gods.

Also a tree of the Fae; sit and watch patiently on midsummer night and you should see the Faerie King ride past.

If an elder self-seeds in your garden it is said that the Earth Mother has chosen to protect your house (don't cut the elder down without asking permission from the Earth Mother first). Preferably, of course, don't cut any trees down at all!

There has been a bit of a dilemma with elder over the years; it has been called a tree of life but also a tree of the devil. It was needed for its medicinal properties but also feared to be a witch's plant – sometimes you just can't win! Witches were said to be able to turn themselves into elder trees… I have yet to attempt it.

The elder is a tree of death, rebirth and reincarnation.

The bark, root, leaves and berries can be used for making dyes.

Use in any healing spell work, whether it is for physical or emotional healing. It is also very good to use to break spells that were cast against you. Elder wands can be used to drive out evil spirits.

Drink elderberry juice to increase your intuition.

Add elderberry tea to your bath water to help heal spiritual and emotional issues.

Add elder stems to incense blends to bring purification and protection to your home.

Elderflower Healing Tea blend

Ingredients
2 heaped teaspoons dried elderflowers
1 teaspoon dried rosemary
250ml / 1 cup / ½ pint boiling water

Pour the boiling water on the herbs and allow them to steep for 5-7 minutes, then strain and either drink or add to your bathwater.

Elderflower Water

You can use this as a skin tonic, but it also works very well as a sacred or blessed water to sprinkle around your property for protection, during purification rituals, to cleanse tools or to use for anointing when working with your intuition or the faerie world.

Ingredients
2 pints (5 cups) elderflowers (fresh, just snip the stalks short)
½ pint (1 cup) boiling water

Use open blossoms and pop them into a large bowl or jug then pour over the boiling water. Leave to infuse for about 3 hours then strain and pour into bottles. Keep in the fridge and it will last about 2 weeks or so.

Elder Magical Properties

Protection, healing, faeries, purification, intuition, exorcism, hex breaking, rebirth.

Ruling Planet: Venus
Sign: Sagittarius, Aquarius, Libra
Element: Water
Gender: Feminine

Elm *(Ulmus campestris)*

This is a graceful tree with distinctive inverted triangles of leaves. It grows throughout most of the Northern Hemisphere and can grow up to 150 feet or more.

The elm balances the heart and energises the mind; it attracts love to you and can help with your psychic powers.

The elm is often found in the Underworld and at crossroads leading to the entrance to the world of the Fae, elves being particularly fond of it.

Wear elm about your person to attract love to you.

Hang a piece of elm over your threshold to bring good luck into the house.

Elm Magical Properties

Love, balance, luck, energy, psychic powers.

Ruling Planet: Saturn, Mercury
Element: Water

Gender: Feminine

Eucalyptus *(Eucalyptus spp)*

Use eucalyptus for any moon workings, but it also works well to bring the energy of the sun into your magic.

Use in incense blends for divination and dream work.

The leaves can be used in healing poppets and medicine pouches whether physical or emotional healing is needed.

The scent is quite cleansing and clearing so I often add it to purification incense blends and it works well burnt in a room after an argument to clear the air.

Eucalyptus Magical Properties

Moon magic, sun magic, divination, dreams, healing, purification.

Ruling Planet: Moon, Sun
Element: Water, Air
Gender: Feminine

Evening Primrose *(Oenothera)*

A species of herbaceous flowering plants that generally have yellow flowers, evening primrose as the name suggests has flowers that open in the evening.

This plant is closely aligned with the moon and has strong feminine energies.

The Faeries love this flower so use in any faerie magic.

Traditionally it was used in hunting rituals and to honour hunting deities, but as we don't often sling a bow and arrow over our shoulders and pop out to catch our dinner these days it can be used in workings to 'hunt down' things such as jobs or relationships.

Evening Primrose Magical Properties

Feminine energy, moon magic, faerie, hunting.

Ruling Planet: Moon
Element: Water
Gender: Feminine

Fennel *(Foeniculum vulgare)*

A perennial, fennel grows up to 5 feet tall with bright green stems that have dark green feathery plumes and bright yellow flowers throughout the summer that turn into aniseed flavour seeds. The root of the plant can also be used and makes a lovely salad or roasted veggie.

One of my favourite spices, it makes a lovely aromatic tea and the seeds can be munched upon after a spicy meal to settle the digestive system and freshen your breath.

It is a fiery spice that brings a breath of fresh, cleansing and purifying air. It is not subtle; it is a strong pungent cleanse, for a real good clear out.

Hang fennel in your house for protection (the seeds in a pouch or the leaves in a bunch… not the fennel bulb because that would just be silly).

Fennel seeds work well in protection, purification and healing spells.

Add fennel seeds to incense blends to cleanse and purify.

You can also add fennel seeds to your bath water to clear your mind and purify your body.

Carry fennel with you for confidence and courage. This probably goes back to Roman soldiers who used to chew the seeds before battle.

Throw fennel seeds at handfastings to ensure fertility for the happy couple. The birds will love you for it as fennel seeds are much tastier than uncooked rice or paper confetti.

Add a few fennel seeds (or a fennel tea bag) to your floor wash to give your home a cleanse and purification and to add protection.

It is another ancient herb that was used to ward against

witches (seriously we are nice people really).

The herb is supposedly effective against snake venom (but I wouldn't recommend it).

Fennel is an excellent seed to use for initiation rituals as it helps to release the old and see clearly the pathway before you, bringing with it courage and protection.

Fennel Magical Properties

Healing, purification, protection, courage, confidence, fertility, initiation.

Ruling Planet: Mercury
Sign: Leo, Virgo, Aquarius
Element: Fire
Gender: Masculine

Fenugreek *(Trigonella foenum-graecum)*

This is an annual herb usually seen in hotter climates, although it can grow in the UK (apparently).

Ewwwww… that is exactly what I think when I get a whiff of fenugreek… it does have an extremely pungent scent. But the seeds are exceptionally good in prosperity pouches and money spells.

Add fenugreek seeds to floor washes to bring in abundance.

Use fenugreek seeds in incense blends to bring blessings to your home.

Place fenugreek seeds under your pillow to stop nightmares.

Use fenugreek for help in psychic protection and grounding and to help focus when you are journeying.

Fenugreek Magical Properties

Prosperity, blessings, money, nightmares, psychic protection, meditation.

Ruling Planet: Mercury
Element: Air

Gender: Masculine

Fern *(Pteridophyte)*

This is a huge category of plants, perennials grown from creeping roots or rhizomes, found in shaded areas usually in woodlands.

Fern is a gateway to the Otherworlds. Use in incense blends to connect with spirit, the Underworld or the world of Faerie.

Have ferns in the house to bring protection and love.

Carrying the seeds is said to make you invisible. Now whilst it won't actually give you superpowers, it can be used in magical workings to help people 'not see you' or 'not take notice of you'.

Fern Magical Properties

Spirit work, Underworld, Faerie, protection, love, invisibility.

Ruling Planet: Mercury
Sign: Taurus, Pisces
Element: Air
Gender: Masculine

Feverfew *(Tanacetum parthenium, Chrysanthemum parthenium)*

Found on roadsides and in hedgerows, feverfew has green hairy leaves and pretty white daisy-like flowers.

Carry feverfew with you to protect against accidents and keep you free from colds and fevers. Use dried feverfew leaves in incense blends to purify the air and bring about a peaceful home.

Feverfew Magical Properties

Protection, peace, health, purification.

Ruling Planet: Venus
Sign: Aries, Sagittarius, Libra
Element: Water
Gender: Masculine

Flax *(Linum usitatissimum)*

An upright annual plant with pretty pale blue flowers, flax is one of the oldest crops. The use of flax in the manufacture of cloth dates back to Neolithic times. The plant provides oil (flaxseed or linseed), fibres for linen and nutritional seeds.

If you can get hold of flax cord it is good to use in knot work magic.

Pop some flax seeds in your purse or wallet to keep the money coming in.

Mix flax seeds with pepper and sprinkle the mixture around your property to keep out negative energy; it will also bring abundance in.

Use flax seeds in healing workings.

Flax Magical Properties

Knot magic, money, protection, healing.

Ruling Planet: Mercury, Venus
Element: Fire
Gender: Masculine

Foxglove *(Digitalis purpurea)*

Foxglove is a biennial plant with tall flower spikes covered in bell-shaped flowers in shades of white, pink and purple. These are beautiful graceful flowers that the bees adore. Grow them in your garden for protection and you will also find them growing in the wild at the entrance to faery mounds. Caution: foxglove is poisonous... do not ingest any part of it.

I think foxglove works very well in stopping gossip spells and 'keeping away the poison' that comes with rumour and tittle tattle.

Use foxglove leaves in workings to attract the help and assistance of the Fae... be careful though... they can be pesky little beggars! (the Fae... not foxgloves).

Foxglove is a plant of the Underworld so works very well for divination and visionary workings.

Foxglove Magical Properties

Protection, gossip, faeries, divination.

Ruling Planet: Venus, Saturn

Element: Water

Gender: Feminine

Frankincense

Frankincense is a resin from the Boswellia tree, a deciduous tree that grows on rocky outcrops.

As with all resins, when burnt on charcoal it makes a lot of smoke, but I have to say I think this is my favourite resin scent. Again, as with most resins, it works well for cleansing and purifying.

It is a good resin to burn for spirituality and your spiritual connection, also for cleansing the chakras and promoting a general feeling of relaxation.

Frankincense can also bring about focus and clarity.

Carry it with you for abundance and to attract love.

Yule Incense Blend

Ingredients
Equal parts of each:
Frankincense
Cinnamon
Pine needles
Cloves

Frankincense Magical Properties

Purification, spirituality, relaxation, focus, love, abundance.

Ruling Planet: Sun

Sign: Aries, Leo, Aquarius

Element: Fire
Gender: Masculine

Garlic *(Allium sativum)*

The garlic that we use is the bulb of the plant that is harvested after the leaves have withered and turned brown, each bulb containing several garlic cloves.

Garlic was used to ward against illness including the plague (useful to know just in case it comes back...).

It is brilliant for absorbing negative energy and evil spirits and of course we all know about the powers of garlic against vampires (I am not too convinced that works though).

Garlic has medicinal and healing properties when eaten, but don't eat too much if you still want lots of kisses.

Hang garlic bulbs over your threshold to keep out unwanted and negative energy; it should also help to keep jealousy out of the home as well.

Eat garlic to give you strength before you have to face a difficult person or enter a trying situation.

Protection Pouch

Ingredients
A black bag / pouch / piece of cloth tied with ribbon
A garlic clove
A star anise
A bay leaf
A pinch of dried nettle
3 black pepper corns

Charge each ingredient with your intent then pop them into the pouch and tie up the top with a ribbon.

Garlic Magical Properties

Exorcism, protection, healing, jealousy, strength.

Ruling Planet: Mars
Sign: Aries
Element: Fire
Gender: Masculine

Geranium *(Pelargonium maculatum / P. odoratissimum / Hortorum)*

Traditionally a witch would grow red geraniums in the garden to ward off negative energies and warn when visitors were coming. I have the vision in my head of the flowers in *Alice in Wonderland*, all turning and shouting to the witch that 'visitors are on the way'.

And before I have all the horticulturists on at me – geranium is a common name we use for the bedding plants we are familiar with, but they are actually officially pelargoniums, geraniums are a huge variety of plants commonly known as cranesbills – confused? Yep, that's why I am using the more common name of geranium here – it's the ones you buy in the garden centre during the summer in pots for your patio. However you can also use the cranesbill varieties as well – same magical properties.

Keep geraniums indoors to make guests feel welcome.

Pink geraniums are good for love spells and white ones for fertility. Adding white geranium petals to incense blends for fertility works very well.

Use geranium petals in spells to help you feel more confident about socialising or to bring more social events your way.

You can also get scented pelargoniums which combine scents such as lemon, peppermint and even chocolate – these can be used very well in spell work.

Use geranium oil to cleanse your aura.

Geranium Magical Properties:

Protection, fertility, love, socialise, aura cleansing.

Ruling Planet: Venus
Sign: Pisces
Element: Water
Gender: Feminine

Ginger *(Zingiber officinale)*

A plant originating in the warmer countries, ginger is a perennial root that creeps and spreads underground. Large green leaves shoot upwards, which are accompanied by yellow or white flowers.

Use ginger in workings to bring about money, prosperity and success and in protective spells. You can also add it to other workings to increase their power.

Wear ginger to bring passion and love to you.

To cleanse and purify, use ginger in an incense blend.

Ginger root can also be used as a poppet. Some of them are very person-shaped but even a straight piece will work well.

Pass your magical tools through incense made from ginger to cleanse, consecrate and add power to them.

Ginger Magical Properties

Money, success, power, love, cleansing, protection, consecrate.

Ruling Planet: Mars
Sign: Aries
Element: Fire
Gender: Masculine

Goldenrod *(Solidago spp)*

An herbaceous perennial grown from a rhizome with tall stems topped with yellow rod-shaped cones of flowers that bloom in late summer.

Have goldenrod flowers indoors to help with meditation and

connecting with your inner knowledge.

Grow goldenrod in your garden to bring you blessings of the magical kind.

Carry goldenrod petals in your purse or wallet to bring money to you.

The flower spikes of goldenrod can be used as divining rods to find water sources or hidden treasure.

Goldenrod Magical Properties

Meditation, knowledge, blessings, money.

Ruling Planet: Venus

Element: Air

Gender: Feminine

Gorse *(Ulex europaeus)*

Gorse is an evergreen shrub that grows on heaths and downlands. It is covered in what seem like spines, but are actually older leaves (the new leaves being soft), and is covered in bright yellow flowers in the spring followed by seed pods.

Gorse is said to attract gold so makes an excellent ingredient in money spells and workings. It is also good for using in protection pouches.

Gorse Magical Properties

Money, protection.

Ruling Planet: Mars

Element: Fire

Gender: Masculine

Gourd *(Cucurbitaceae)*

I can remember my dad growing ornamental gourds in his allotment when we were children, weird looking shapes, sizes and patterns, but all beautiful in their own funny way. Most of them are only ornamental though so don't be tempted to eat them.

Carry dried pieces of gourd with you or place them above your front door to bring protection.

Hollowed out and filled with dried peas or beans they make brilliant rattles to clear away negative energy.

Gourd Rattle

Pick a suitable shaped gourd and cut off the small end then scrape out the inside. This may not be easy; try using a knife and a spoon. You must scrape away all of the membrane that is inside otherwise it is liable to go mouldy.

Leave your gourd in a dry, warm area – it may take a couple of months to be properly dry. If you are totally impatient (like me) you can speed up the process by drying the gourd out in an oven on a really low temperature – don't burn it!

Place a handful of dried peas or dried beans into the gourd – different dried pulses or seeds will make different noises.

You can either now just plug the hole with loads of glue, or seal it with cork and glue the edges. Alternatively you can insert a piece of wooden dowel to make a handle and seal the join with glue – this part takes a bit of creativity.

You can leave the gourd natural coloured or paint and varnish it.

Gourd Magical Properties

Protection, cleansing.

Ruling Planet: Moon
Element: Water
Gender: Masculine

Grass (*Graminoids*)

Yep grass… the green stuff you have in your lawn, on roadsides, in the park… well pretty much everywhere really. I know it might seem common and boring, but it still has magical properties.

If you have the patience you can 'weave' a ball of grass and hang it up in your home to provide protection; you can also plait the longer stems to make witches' ladders.

Use long blades of grass for knot magic.

Use grass in incense blends to increase your psychic powers and bring abundance your way.

Grass Magical Properties
Protection, psychic powers, knot magic, abundance.
Element: Earth

Hawthorn *(Crataegus oxyacantha / monogyna)*
A hedgerow plant that grows well even in poor soil and high winds. It has white flowers in spring that are followed by dark red berries in the autumn. Watch out for the spiky thorns though!

Associated with easing heart complaints I think it works well in love workings and spells to make the heart sing with happiness (awwwwww).

Hawthorn is a tree of the Fae, forming the faery triad with oak and ash. The hawthorn offers a gateway to the world of faerie.

The white flowers followed by the red berries have long been associated with fertility.

May Day circlets are often made of hawthorn, adding more weight to its fertility properties.

Dry hawthorn berries and thread onto black cotton and hang above your threshold or sprinkle the berries around the boundary to your home for protection.

Add hawthorn berries to your floor wash to purify your house.

Add it to workings where you require forgiveness.

Use hawthorn in workings for protection, hope and warding against evil... yes another tree that protects against witches (sigh), although apparently witches would shapeshift into hawthorn trees to rest before flying through the night.

Happy Hawthorn Leaf Tea
Mix equal quantities of your usual black tea and dried hawthorn leaves. Add hot water and allow it to steep for 3-5 minutes then strain and drink to bring love to your heart and a smile to your face.

Hawthorn Magical Properties
Happiness, fertility, love, protection, purification, forgiveness, faeries, hope.
Ruling Planet: Mars, Venus
Sign: Sagittarius
Element: Fire
Gender: Masculine

Hazel *(Corylus spp. avellana, Corylus cornuta)*
Hazel is a small tree commonly found in woods and hedges. The bark is shiny and smooth and the leaves are asymmetrical oval shapes. Towards the end of winter yellow catkins appear and in autumn we get hazelnuts.

Hazel wands are excellent for all uses, but especially for healing.

To bring in the magic of the Fae, hang hazelnuts up in your home.

Use hazel in workings for knowledge, wisdom and inspiration.

Wear a crown made from hazel twigs to make your wishes a reality.

Wrap hazel catkins in red or pink paper or twine, light from a pink or red candle then drop in a cauldron (or other fireproof container) and visualise your true love coming to you as you do so.

For couples who wish to know if they are well suited, each

take a hazel nut and drop them into the embers of a fire. If the nuts burn evenly and steadily next to each other than the match is a good one. However, if the nuts jump and pop away from each other the relationship is not meant to be... or so they say...

Keep a few hazel nuts on your altar to bring prosperity and wisdom.

Hazel makes excellent dowsing rods. Using a forked twig, the dowser can be used to find water and concealed objects. Hold the ends of the forked twig in each hand and walk forwards, when the forked point dips you have found...something!

Hazel Magical Properties
Fertility, wishes, love, protection, luck, wisdom, divination, healing, inspiration, prosperity.

Ruling Planet: Sun
Element: Air
Gender: Masculine

Heather *(Calluna spp, Erica spp, vulgaris)*
Found mostly on moors, hillsides, heaths and boggy places where the soil is acidic, heather has tiny narrow, spiky evergreen leaves and pink, purple or white flowers in late summer. It is a delicacy that sheep like to munch on where there isn't much else on the hillside.

"Buy some lucky heather my dear?"

Heather has been associated with luck for years, white heather is best for luck. It is a lovely cleansing flower to use to clear sacred space. It can also be used in spells to bring rain and conjure ghosts (should you wish to). To bring about rain, burn some heather in an incense blend.

Bunch together some longish stems of heather to make a small 'broom' for clearing and cleansing ritual circles and sacred space.

Pink heather works well for love and friendship spell work and purple is excellent for any kind of spirit work. It is also said to open a portal between this world and the world of faerie. Heather also aids in shape shifting with the actual transformation and protection whilst you are in another form.

Drop a few heather flowers into your floor wash to cleanse, purify and protect your home.

Heather Pillows

Heather makes a very cushy comfy bed (so I am told) and can be made into pillows to use whilst lounging in the garden and lying on the grass. It could provide some interesting dreams and journeys... Cut a bundle of heather and tie it into small bunches then hang them up to dry. Cut out the really hard and woody stems, then stuff the heather into small pillow cases. Felt would work well as it doesn't require hemming, but cotton or canvas is good too.

Heather Magical Properties

Luck, protection, cleansing, ghosts, rain, spirit, love, friendship, faeries, dreams, shape shifting.

Ruling Planet: Venus

Element: Water

Gender: Feminine

Heliotrope *(Heliotropium spp)*

This is a huge genus of flowering plants in the borage family ranging from those considered weeds to decorative garden plants. Butterflies love the fragrant purple flowers, but be careful with dogs near the plants; they can be toxic if eaten.

Place the flowers beneath your bed for prophetic dreams.

Meditate with the flowers near to assist you with your spiritual connection.

Sprinkle the flowers around your home and use them in incense blends to keep out and banish negative energy.

Use in workings for forgiveness for yourself and from others.

Keep heliotrope flowers in your purse or wallet to attract abundance.

Heliotrope Magical Properties

Dreams, spirituality, exorcism, protection, forgiveness, abundance.

Ruling Planet: Sun
Sign: Leo
Element: Fire
Gender: Masculine

Holly *(Ilex aquifolium, Ilex opaca)*

Holly is an evergreen shrub that can grow into a tree if left to its own devices. It has dark glossy green leaves and red berries during winter. It wouldn't be Yule without holly would it? However, holly is also burnt at Imbolc ceremonies.

Keep a sprig of holly above your bed to ensure good dreams and insightful visions.

Plant holly around your property for protection against lightning, poison and evil spirits.

Put holly sprigs on your altar at the winter solstice to invite happiness, balance, success and luck into your life for the coming year.

The holly berry is symbolic of the life giving blood of the Goddess. To work with fertility and feminine sexuality take three holly berries and throw them in water (the ocean, a river or a pond) and make your request to deity as you do so.

Holly Magical Properties

Protection, luck, dreams, balance, success.

Ruling Planet: Mars, Saturn
Element: Fire
Gender: Masculine

Honesty *(Lunaria spp)*

An annual or biennial growing fairly tall with large pointed leaves bearing white or purple flowers in spring and summer followed by translucent disc-shaped seed pods.

Carry honesty flowers or seeds with you to keep monsters at bay (I haven't tried this yet...).

The seed pods look like coins so they are excellent to use in money spells or just pop one in your purse or wallet to ensure it is never empty – well it won't be... because there will always be a seed pod in it!

Honesty also does what it says on the tin... use it in workings to make sure you are being told the truth.

Honesty Magical Properties

Money, monsters, truth.

Ruling Planet: Moon

Element: Earth

Gender: Feminine

Honeysuckle *(Lonicera caprifolium, Lonicera japonica, Lonicera periclymenum)*

Honeysuckle is a beautiful climbing plant to grow in your garden with sweet scented white, yellow and red flowers throughout spring and summer followed by berries in the autumn that the birds love. It also grows in the wild, usually in heavily wooded areas.

Apparently it was once thought far too dangerous to bring honeysuckle flowers into the house because the scent would cause young ladies to become 'unnecessary' and given to 'forbidden thoughts'... seems to me like a definite flower to keep indoors...

Dab honeysuckle oil on your forehead to promote quick thinking and boost your memory. This also helps to increase your psychic powers.

Use honeysuckle flowers in all prosperity and money workings.

Honeysuckle can be added to other herbs in magical workings to help balance the blend and aid in the effectiveness of the intent.

Use in incense blends to help you meditate, increase your psychic powers and connect with spirit.

Honeysuckle Magical Properties

Prosperity, psychic powers, protection, balance, lust, meditation, memory.

Ruling Planet: Jupiter
Sign: Gemini, Cancer
Element: Earth
Gender: Masculine

Horehound *(Marrubium vulgare)*

A bushy perennial plant with wrinkly leaves and fluffy hairs, horehound has white flowers throughout the summer.

Originally used to protect against witches and their evil ways (yep another one), it works as protection against negative energy.

Ancient Egyptians dedicated this plant to Horus and often referred to it as the 'seed of Horus'.

Use it in incense blends to help you focus and bring clarity to your thoughts.

Keep horehound in the house to bring peace and love to your home.

Wear horehound on you to aid with healing.

Horehound Magical Properties

Exorcism, protection, healing, clarity, peace, love.

Ruling Planet: Mercury
Sign: Scorpio
Element: Air

Gender: Masculine

Horseradish *(Cochlearia armoracia, Armoracia rusticana)*

Horseradish is a perennial with bright green dock-like leaves that have wavy edges (and quite often lots of holes because the snails love them). Tresses of white flowers occasionally appear in the summer. The magic of the plant, however, is found in the root. Be careful because once you have it in your garden it is difficult to remove. The name 'horse' actually means 'coarse' or 'rough'.

It is not just used to make a hot relish to accompany roast beef…

Hang horseradish over your doorway to keep out negative energies and protect against hexes.

Place a piece of horseradish at each corner of your property to bring in luck and abundance.

Horseradish on your altar or burnt in an incense blend can help with focus for your meditations.

Carry horseradish with you to give you strength.

Horseradish Magical Properties

Exorcism, purification, strength, meditation, hexes, luck, abundance.

Ruling Planet: Mars
Sign: Aries
Element: Fire
Gender: Masculine

Horsetail *(Equisetum arvense, Equisetum telmateia)*

Horsetail is a leafless and non-flowering perennial plant that has tall hollow jointed stems that are covered in green 'teeth' and can be found on roadsides, waste ground and in gardens.

This plant is ancient, seriously ancient. Relatives have been found from roughly 270-370 million years ago... see I said it was old...

The name 'equisetum' means 'horse' or 'bristle'. The Romans used to call it 'hair of the earth'.

The plant was sold right up until the 18th century as a scourer for pewter and to clean wood and glass.

Apparently (no I haven't tried it) you can make a whistle out of the stem of horsetail; playing the whistle will enchant snakes.

Use horsetail in fertility pouches and amulets or keep some in the bedroom to increase fertility chances.

As it is such an ancient plant and has survived so many centuries it makes sense that this plant would work very well in any workings that require longevity.

Horsetail works well if you need strength of will power or to define boundaries in a relationship or situation.

Use it in workings that require letting go of the old and cleansing of any past troubles linked to your emotions.

Horsetail Magical Properties

Fertility, snakes, longevity, strength, cleansing.

Ruling Planet: Saturn
Element: Earth
Gender: Feminine

Hyacinth (*Hyacinthus orientalis*)

A bulb that produces highly scented very pretty flowers on stems that come up from between long green leaves in early spring. Hyacinths come in all sorts of colours; purple, pink, white and yellow.

The scent of the hyacinth (which can be very potent) can bring about a sense of peace, happiness and calm (or hayfever...).

Keep a hyacinth in your bedroom to ensure a good sleep and to keep nightmares away.

Use dried hyacinth petals in spell work for love and

abundance.

Hyacinth Magical Properties
Love, happiness, peace, sleep, nightmares, abundance.
Ruling Planet: Venus
Element: Water
Gender: Feminine

Hyssop (*Hyssopus officinalis*)
This is a woody base shrub with dark green leaves producing bunches of pink, blue or occasionally white flowers during the summer.

It is an excellent herb to use for purification and protection.

Hang a sprig of hyssop above your doorway to keep out negative energy. You can also tie a few hyssop sprigs together to make a besom to sweep out negative energy.

Add a handful of dried hyssop to your floor wash water to cleanse your home or add to your bathwater to heal and purify.

During the Dark Ages this herb was strewn on the floor in houses of those who were suffering from illness. You probably don't want it all over your carpet, but it works well in healing pouches and incense blends.

Hyssop Magical Properties
Purification, protection, healing.
Ruling Planet: Jupiter, Moon
Sign: Cancer
Element: Fire
Gender: Masculine

Iris (*Iris spp*)
Irises are perennial plants grown from creeping rhizomes (such a good name for a rock band) or bulbs, a huge species of flowering plants. The name 'iris' comes from the Greek word for

rainbow. The iris bulb is also referred to as orris root.

This is most definitely a moon plant; use iris for any kind of moon magic including divination and dream work.

Also use iris to draw love to you. In Hoodoo the root of the iris is called the Queen Elizabeth root and is referred to as the 'love drawing herb'.

Bring iris flowers into the house to cleanse and purify the energies.

The iris flower symbolises faith, wisdom and valour.

Iris Magical Properties

Wisdom, purification, moon magic, divination, dreams, love.

Ruling Planet: Moon, Venus
Sign: Taurus, Aquarius
Element: Water
Gender: Feminine

Ivy *(Hedera helix)*

Ivy is an evergreen climbing or ground creeping plant with dark green leaves.

Ivy creeps, clings and binds as it grows so it is ideal for binding spells.

Make an ivy wreath to place in your home to bring love and abundance in and to keep negative energy out.

Use ivy in workings for protection, fidelity and healing.

Ladies should carry ivy with them for good luck (sorry guys, this seems to be a feminine thing).

Ivy is a symbol of the Goddess and feminine energy; it also represents the spiral of life.

Ivy Magical Properties

Protection, healing, binding, love, abundance, fidelity.

Ruling Planet: Saturn, Moon
Sign: Scorpio

Element: Water
Gender: Feminine

Jasmine (*Jasminum grandiflorum, Jasminum officinale, Jasminum odoratissimum*)

Jasmine is a very pretty climbing plant with white, yellow and sometimes pink flowers (I have the pink variety in my garden) with a delightful scent. I also occasionally get the white jasmine growing in my garden as it climbs over the wall from next door.

Use jasmine flowers in money, prosperity and abundance workings, along with peace and love magic.

Have a jasmine plant nearby when you meditate as the scent helps with your spiritual connection.

Have jasmine in your home or garden to bring in balance, abundance, peace and love.

Also add jasmine flowers to workings and incense blends to spice up your sex life.

Associated with the moon, jasmine also works well in any moon magic spells.

Spicy Love Life Jasmine Iced Tea

Ingredients
3 tablespoons jasmine tea (or you can use a tea bag of jasmine tea)
2 tablespoons honey
1 cinnamon stick
4 cups boiling water
1 ¼ cups of sparkling water

You can make up your own jasmine tea, which is dried jasmine flowers mixed with either a black or green tea leaf, but I find it much easier to use already blended jasmine tea in a bag.

Pour the boiling water onto the tea, add the honey and stir

well then drop the cinnamon stick in and leave to steep. When it is cool, add the sparkling water and you can chuck in a couple of ice cubes if you wish.

Jasmine Magical Properties

Dreams, money, love, meditation, lust.

Ruling Planet: Moon, Venus
Sign: Cancer
Element: Water
Gender: Feminine

Juniper (*Juniperus communis*)

An evergreen shrub that can spread or grow upright depending on location, juniper has short spiny tipped leaves and yellow flowers in early summer that turn into green berry cones, which then ripen to the dark purple juniper berries we are familiar with.

It is another herb that is old as the hills, dating back to Neolithic times apparently (personally I don't remember that far back).

Keep a sprig of juniper above the door for protection and to keep negative energy out. It has very strong protective properties that keep out all sorts of evil demons.

If you have had something stolen you can petition the spirit of the juniper bush to bring the article back to you and justice to be served.

Wear juniper berries in an amulet to bring love to you and to keep you healthy, also use it in healing workings.

Use it in incense blends to purify and cleanse, bring clarity and also to aid with psychic powers. Juniper has strong connections to the spirit world and the afterlife.

Juniper also works well in moon magic, on the dark of the moon.

Juniper Magical Properties

Love, exorcism, healing, protection, justice, stolen items, purification, psychic powers, clarity.

Ruling Planet: Sun, Jupiter, Moon
Sign: Aries
Element: Fire
Gender: Masculine

Knotweed *(Polygonum aviculare)*

A straggling plant found along roadsides with tiny pink / white flowers.

Tell this plant all your troubles and worries let it take them from you… then burn it to remove them.

Carry with you to improve your health, vision and clarity.

Works incredibly well in binding spells and in spell work to 'keep things together'.

Knotweed Magical Properties

Binding, health, clarity, worries

Ruling Planet: Saturn
Element: Earth
Gender: Feminine

Lady's Mantle *(Alchemilla spp)*

This is a perennial plant grown from rhizomes, with green fan-shaped leaves and clusters of small flowers in the spring and summer.

Lady's mantle has a very feminine energy and is a plant ruled by Venus and the element of water so absolutely perfect to use in any love magic.

Lady's Mantle Magical Properties

Love.

Ruling Planet: Venus

Sign: Scorpio
Element: Water
Gender: Feminine

Lavender *(Lavandula officinalis or Lavandula vera)*

Lavender is an evergreen shrub with lilac colour flowers that grow on top of tall spikes. The leaves are small, narrow and a greyish colour. They bring with them a beautiful scent during June and September when they flower, but even when dried the flowers retain their smell.

Apparently Roman 'ladies of the night' used the scent of lavender to attract customers… just in case you needed a bit of cash.

Lavender sharpens your mind and gives clarity to your thoughts.

It is a faerie flower and also used in love workings (not the hot passionate love affair type, more the Jane Austen romance type).

Use lavender flowers in sleep spells or make a lavender pillow to help you get a restful night's sleep.

Lavender is a very calming, peaceful herb and can be used in workings with that intent. It will also bring calm, happiness and tranquillity. Try adding a handful of lavender buds to your bath water.

Hang a bunch of lavender over your threshold to bring peace to your home and to keep out negative energy.

Lavender can be worn to protect against emotional abuse, to banish negative words and give you inner strength.

I also use lavender in my smudge sticks together with sage and rosemary.

If you pick your own or are able to get hold of lavender on long stems it can be used to create all sorts of beautiful crafts; tie a handful together to create a small lavender besom or make five small bundles and tie together in a pentacle shape.

Lavender Harmony Tea

Ingredients
2 teaspoons lavender buds
1 tablespoon white rose petals
1 teaspoon violet petals
1 ½ cups apple juice
1 cinnamon stick

Simmer all the ingredients together for 5-10 minutes then strain out the petals and cinnamon stick. Drink whilst visualising love, harmony and peace.

Lavender Magical Properties

Happiness, peace, love, protection, sleep, clarity, faeries, strength.

Ruling Planet: Mercury
Sign: Leo, Gemini
Element: Air
Gender: Masculine

Lemon Balm *(Melissa officinalis)*

This herb grows like a wild thing in my garden. I have had to confine it to pots otherwise it would take over! The bees absolutely love it even though the flowers are tiny, which makes it an excellent herb to use in bee magic and it self-seeds all over the place.

I think it looks a little bit like mint (probably because it is of the same family), but it has a beautiful lemon scent and flavour when you crush the leaves.

The Elizabethans apparently favoured lemon balm in food and drink, not only for its taste but also because it was said to relieve depression and aid in a good memory so I use it in sachets, medicine pouches and powders for both intents.

Lemon balm works really well in any success, healing or love workings.

Carry lemon balm with you to ease anxiety and bring about balance and calm.

Take a lemon balm leaf and wish for happiness upon it, leave the leaf to dry on your altar or beside your bed until it has worked its magic, then burn the leaf and send a blessing of thanks.

And just in case... lemon balm is apparently very good for healing sword wounds... not that you get many of those nowadays, but it is always best to be prepared.

Uplifting Lemon Balm Tea

Ingredients
Lemon balm leaves (a good handful)
Two strips lemon peel
Half a cinnamon stick
Pinch of nutmeg
Half a teaspoon of coriander seeds

Place all the ingredients in a teapot and add boiling water. Allow to steep for 5 minutes, then strain and pour.

This mixture also makes a good blend to add to your bath water (two tablespoons of the steeped liquid).

Lemon Balm Magical Properties
Success, healing, anti depression, memory, love, anxiety.
Ruling Planet: Moon, Venus
Sign: Cancer
Element: Water
Gender: Feminine

Lemon Verbena (*Aloysia citrodora*)

This is a perennial shrub with pointed glossy lemon scented leaves; lilac or white flowers appear in late spring / early summer.

Place lemon verbena leaves under your pillow to stop nightmares.

Add it to incense blends to dispel negative energy, cleanse and purify.

Add it to love magic workings.

Lemon Verbena Magical Properties

Nightmares, purification, exorcism, love.

Ruling Planet: Mercury
Sign: Pisces
Element: Air
Gender: Masculine

Lilac (*Syringa vulgaris*)

Lilac is a perennial bush with traditionally purple colour flowers for a few weeks in the spring, but they also come in shades of white, red and pink. The blossom has a beautiful scent.

Wear lilac petals in an amulet or medicine pouch to attract love to you and provide personal protection.

Sprinkle lilac petals around your property to keep out negative energy.

Burn lilac petals in incense blends to aid your meditations and strengthen your spiritual connection.

Lilac Magical Properties

Protection, exorcism, love, meditation.

Ruling Planet: Venus
Element: Water
Gender: Feminine

Lily *(Lilium spp)*

Tall perennial flowering plants grown from bulbs (be careful as some of them can be poisonous).

Lily is one of my favourite flowers, so beautiful and graceful, but be careful with the pollen because it stains.

It is a very feminine flower associated with both the moon and Venus so works well for any Goddess work, especially the Goddess of witchcraft, Lilith.

Use in protection, hexes and uncrossing spell work.

Lily Magical Properties:

Goddess, witchcraft, hexes, uncrossing, protection.

Ruling Planet: Moon, Venus
Sign: Scorpio
Element: Water
Gender: Feminine

Lily of the Valley *(Convallaria majalis)*

This is a pretty, quite small, but fragrant plant with broad green leaves and tiny white bell-shaped flowers. The shoots start to show in the spring followed by the flowers and then in early autumn they are followed by red berries.

Add lily of the valley to incense or bath water to cleanse your energy and bring about happiness.

Plant lily of the valley in your garden to bring happiness and success into your home and to provide protection.

The flowers look like tiny cups so this plant is associated with the Fae. The flowers are said to ring and are used as ladders by the Fae. Use lily of the valley to attract faeries to your property.

Folklore says that lily of the valley blooms on the grave of a person who was executed for a crime they are innocent of committing.

Use lily of the valley in workings and incense to help with your divination skills and magical powers.

Lily of the Valley Magical Properties

Happiness, cleansing, success, faeries, divination, magic.

Ruling Planet: Mercury
Sign: Pisces
Element: Air
Gender: Masculine

Lobelia *(Lobelia spp)*

Lobelia is a huge genus of annual and perennial flowering plants. The most commonly used lobelia in magical workings is *Lobelia inflata.*

It is a very feminine plant so works well in all kinds of love magic.

Throw dried lobelia towards a storm to stop it from coming any closer.

Lobelia siphilitica is good to use in incense blends for purification and protection against psychic attacks.

Lobelia Magical Properties

Love, weather magic, protection, purification.

Ruling Planet: Saturn, Neptune
Element: Water
Gender: Feminine

Lovage *(Levisticum officinale)*

Lovage is a tall perennial plant the leaves of which are used as an herb, the root as a vegetable and the seeds as a spice – nothing like making the most of a plant! Yellow flowers are produced in late spring followed by seeds in the autumn.

Hang lovage above your door or window to keep negative energy out.

The name 'lovage' says what it does on the tin – love – so use it in all magical love workings.

Lovage Magical Properties

Protection, love.

Ruling Planet: Sun, Moon
Sign: Taurus
Element: Fire
Gender: Masculine

Lungwort *(Pulmonaria officinalis)*

This is a pretty clump-forming evergreen / herbaceous perennial plant covered in bristly hairs with large oval leaves that are often covered in white spots (part of the plant colouration not because it didn't wash properly…). The flowers are purple, violet, blue or pink. It is a common plant found in the wild and a member of the borage family (the leaves look a bit similar). The leaves were used medicinally as a pulmonary herb because the leaves 'resemble lung tissue'.

Because of its history with healing it makes a good magical healing herb too.

It also works well for medicine pouches and incense blends to clear, cleanse and release any emotional blockages or situations where there is a stalemate.

Add it to incense blends to bring about a calm and soothing energy to your home.

Lungwort Magical Properties

Healing, cleansing, releasing, calming.

Ruling Planet: Mercury
Sign: Taurus, Pisces
Element: Earth
Gender: Masculine

Mace *(Myristica fragrans)*

Mace is the covering that surrounds the spice nutmeg. Mace has a more delicate flavour and scent than nutmeg.

Use it in incense blends to purify and consecrate ritual space. Add it to incense blends to increase your psychic powers.

Mace Magical Properties

Purification, consecration, psychic powers.

Ruling Planet: Mercury, Sun
Sign: Sagittarius
Element: Air
Gender: Masculine

Magnolia *(Magnolia spp)*

This is an ancient flowering tree that apparently appeared even before bees existed.

I think this flower is very feminine, but also has an incredible earthy element to it so would work well in any Mother Earth workings.

It is also used in fidelity spells.

Magnolia Magical Properties

Earth magic, fidelity.

Ruling Planet: Venus
Element: Earth
Gender: Feminine

Mallow *(Malva spp, Lavatera)*

This covers a huge genus of plants (*Lavatera* being a part of the *Malvaceae* family), all flowering, and includes annual, biennial and perennial plants and shrubs. Marsh mallows are rarely found in the wild now. If you do, please resist the urge to pick them, instead grow cultivated ones in your garden.

With all the water connection, feminine energy and being ruled by the moon and Venus, this plant just shouts out to be used in all love magic workings.

It does, however, also have a connection with the dead and is often used in Samhain rituals and is also good for protection spell work.

Mallow Protection Incense Blend

Ingredients
2 parts mallow (flowers and leaves)
2 parts rosemary
1 part thyme

Mallow Magical Properties

Love, Samhain, protection.
Ruling Planet: Moon, Venus
Element: Water
Gender: Feminine

Mandrake *(Mandragora officinarum)*

It's poisonous... enough said.

It is the root of the mandrake that is used in magical workings. The root often resembles the shape of a body so makes it also useful as a poppet. The leaves are ovate and wrinkled, and white or purple flowers are produced followed by orange berries. The only part of the mandrake that is not poisonous is the fruit.

The roots can be kept as a household protection poppet. Wrap them in silk or satin and anoint them with alcohol or oil every so often. You may also like to leave your mandrake poppet offerings occasionally (chocolate or silver coins work well)... I respond well to the same type of offerings... Feeding and tending to your poppet will also bring love and prosperity to your household.

You can also carry a piece of mandrake root with you for personal protection and to attract love to you.

Mandrake Magical Properties

Protection, love, prosperity.

Ruling Planet: Mercury
Sign: Taurus, Cancer, Virgo
Element: Fire
Gender: Masculine

Marigold *(Calendula officinalis)*

Marigold is an annual bedding plant with lots of different varieties (different species), but all have gold, yellow and orange flowers that have a strong scent. It is said that slugs don't like the taste... whoever said it was lying... I have the proof.

Marigold is my plant of choice whenever I am putting together any spells or incense blends for psychic powers.

Put marigold flowers under your bed to ensure a good sleep and keep away nightmares and invite in prophetic dreams.

Place marigold flowers around your house and hang them over doorways for protection and to fill your home with positive energy.

With the bright, cheerful colours and the energy of the sun, marigold makes a good herb to use for happiness and uplifting workings.

Carry marigold with you to bring you luck, especially in legal cases or for gamblers.

Mix with bay leaf and use the mix in anti-gossip workings.

Reveal Marigold Tea

Drink to boost your psychic powers.

Ingredients
1 pint apple juice
½ cup of sugar
Two tablespoons marigold flowers
1 orange, sliced
4 geranium petals

Warm all the ingredients together for 7-10 minutes on a low heat until the sugar has dissolved. Strain and keep chilled. Drink cold with ice or re-heat to serve warm.

Marigold Magical Properties

Psychic powers, dreams, protection, luck, happiness, gossip.

Ruling Planet: Sun
Sign: Leo
Element: Fire
Gender: Masculine

Marjoram *(Origanum majorana)*

I grow several varieties of marjoram in my garden, but it also grows in the wild on dry grassland and waste ground. The plant is a perennial growing up to 2 feet high with slender stems and small oval leaves. Lilac coloured flowers appear in the summer. It is often referred to as sweet or knotted marjoram.

Greeks and Romans wove garlands of marjoram for betrothed couples to wear, making it an excellent herb to use in love workings and marriage spells. Put a bundle of marjoram under your pillow to dream of your future love.

It is a happy herb and can be used in happiness and anti-depression spell work very successfully; it is also good for aiding with grief.

Sprinkle marjoram leaves around your house for protection. Hang a bunch over your threshold for the same purpose.

Add a sprinkle of marjoram to your bath water to help you stay healthy and to keep bugs at bay.

It is also very nice in pasta sauce.

Marjoram Magical Properties

Love, happiness, health, protection, marriage, grief.

Ruling Planet: Mercury
Sign: Aries, Capricorn

Element: Air
Gender: Masculine

Meadowsweet *(Spiraea filipendula, Filipendula ulmaria, Spiraea ulmaria)*

This is a perennial with serrated leaves that are a silver colour underneath and scented creamy white flowers in summer. It can be found in marshes, streams, ditches and some woodlands.

An herb that smells of freshly mown grass, meadowsweet reminds me of summer and skipping through daisy filled meadows (OK I don't actually get to do that much but the thought is there). It has a really happy, blissful and peaceful energy.

My research guides me to the suggestion that the name 'meadow' is more to do with the drink mead than grassy meadows (which is always a good thing), the flowers of meadowsweet having been used for centuries to flavour mead, wine and beer.

Keep meadowsweet in the house to ensure a happy and peaceful home.

Use in love, peace and happiness spell work.

(Caution: If you are allergic to aspirin you may find the same with meadowsweet).

A Cup of Sunshine and Happiness

Ingredients
4 fresh flowering heads of meadowsweet
4 leaves from the top of the plant
250ml / 1 cup / ½ pint boiling water

Bruise the flowers lightly (with a wooden spoon) then pour on the boiling water, cover and allow it to steep for 5-7 minutes, strain then drink hot. You shouldn't need any sweetener. This is also nice chilled with lots of ice and a dash of lemon juice.

You can use dried meadowsweet flowers, but the taste is not as sweet. Use two teaspoons of dried meadowsweet flowers.

Meadowsweet Magical Properties

Peace, happiness, love.

Ruling Planet: Jupiter

Sign: Gemini, Pisces

Element: Air

Gender: Masculine

Mint *(Mentha spp, Mentha aquatica, Mentha piperita)*

Mint is an aromatic perennial with dense lilac flowers, usually grown in gardens but can be found in the wild beside streams and in damp woodlands. There are a huge amount of varieties.

I have it in my garden, but keep it restricted in a pot otherwise it would take over the world. You have been warned.

Use peppermint oil on your forehead and the corners of your books (yeah I know, I can't bring myself to put it on my books either) to aid concentration.

Drinking mint tea can help with keeping communications sweet.

The scent is uplifting and positive and can also be used in travel spells.

Mint can be cooling so I think it works well in spell work to 'cool down' a situation.

Add a few sprigs of fresh mint to a glass of water to cleanse and purify your body from the inside out.

Add mint to your floor wash to clear and cleanse the home.

Place peppermint leaves under your pillow for a calm and restful sleep.

Keep a mint leaf in your purse or wallet to ensure money keeps coming in.

Peppermint has lots of cooling and calming medicinal

properties so use it in healing spells too.

Sprinkle mint around your property to provide protection from negative energy.

Mint Magical Properties

Money, healing, exorcism, protection, cleansing, calming.

Ruling Planet: Mercury, Venus

Sign: Gemini, Taurus, Cancer, Leo, Aquarius

Element: Air

Gender: Masculine

Mistletoe *(Viscum album, Phoradendron leucarpum, Phoradendron flavescens)*

This evergreen plant is considered parasitic because it lives on other plants (trees). It is often found on apple, ash and hawthorn and occasionally on oak trees. Mistletoe has long thin green leaves with small flowers in May followed by white berries in December.

As mistletoe doesn't have roots in the earth but seemingly appears to grow 'from the air' in trees, it is considered a sacred plant from the 'in between' places.

Hang mistletoe in your home for protection and to bring love and peace to your household.

Use mistletoe in fertility, dream and healing spell work, especially for spiritual healing.

Why do we kiss under mistletoe? In Norse mythology the arrow that killed Baldur was made from mistletoe. The Norse gods then ruled that mistletoe belonged to the Goddess of love as a balance for its use to kill – possibly an explanation of why we now kiss under it. Or it could be that mistletoe was used at the Roman festival of Saturnalia in wedding ceremonies ... any excuse is good with me.

Wands made of mistletoe are said to ward off werewolves. I have not tried this as we don't get many werewolves where I

live…
Caution: Mistletoe is poisonous – do not ingest it.

Mistletoe Magical Properties
Fertility, protection, love, health, dreams.
Ruling Planet: Sun
Sign: Leo
Element: Air
Gender: Masculine

Morning Glory *(Convolvulaceae, Ipomoea)*
Usually perennial but in colder areas grown as annuals, climbing or trailing, morning glory has pretty flowers that open and bloom in the early morning.

Use the seeds and flowers for divination and add to incense blends to increase your psychic abilities and astral travel skills.

Morning Glory Magical Properties
Divination, astral travel, psychic powers.
Ruling Planet: Sun, Neptune
Element: Air
Gender: Masculine

Mugwort *(Artemisia vulgaris)*
This is a tall perennial with silvery flower spikes and dark green leaves with silver underneath found on roadsides and waste ground. Collect the flowers when they are open or just before, and the leaves as well.

Mugwort is a very ancient herb for healing, magic and divination known to be protective to women and travellers.

The Latin name *Artemisia* comes from Artemis the Greek moon Goddess and patron of women, so it is an excellent herb to use for feminine energy and issues.

A bundle of mugwort placed under your pillow will bring

about peaceful sleep and aid with lucid dreams and astral travel.

Mugwort makes a good alternative to sage in smudge sticks for cleansing and clearing.

Carry mugwort with you to provide psychic protection and use it in workings to increase your psychic powers.

Throw mugwort onto the fire at midsummer to ensure protection for the following year.

Mugwort does not seem to be particularly favoured by the Fae so if you want to keep them out hang a bunch over your threshold.

A wash made with mugwort (dried mugwort steeped in boiling water) can be used to cleanse your crystals and tools or added to your floor wash. Drink mugwort tea to help with your divination skills.

Place mugwort in your shoes to gain strength and stamina.

Mugwort Smudge Stick

Pick the top few inches of mugwort preferably when the flowers are still in bud (but not essential). Leave them to dry for a few days, then bundle them up before they are completely dry. Tie the ends together by winding a piece of twine or cotton around in a spiral from the base up to the top and back down again. Tie this securely then leave it to dry out completely.

To use, hold the smudge stick at the stem end and light the tip. It might need a little persuasion to get going; this can be done by gently blowing on it. As you wave the smudge stick around each room / person, the air circulating should keep it alight.

Mugwort Magical Properties

Strength, psychic powers, protection, dreams, healing, astral travel, feminine energy, cleansing.

Ruling Planet: Venus, Moon
Sign: Cancer
Element: Earth

Gender: Feminine

Mullein *(Verbascum)*

This large group of biennial or perennial plants has a rosette of leaves and a central tall stem with usually yellow flowers. The mullein leaf used in herbalism is usually *Verbascum thapsus*.

It is a very good protective herb that was placed under butter churns to bring back butter that the witches had magically removed... It is also said to bring back children that were stolen by the Fae.

Pop mullein into dream pillows to prevent nightmares.

Use it in incense blends to help you centre and focus.

It is also occasionally used instead of graveyard dirt in magical workings. I am not sure that there is a 'substitute' for graveyard dirt, but it would certainly work very well in its place. Go with your intuition on this one.

Mullein Magical Properties

Protection, nightmares, centring.

Ruling Planet: Saturn, Mercury
Sign: Aquarius
Element: Fire
Gender: Feminine

Mustard *(Brassica / Sinapis)*

The mustard seeds we use as spice, grinding them and mixing with water and vinegar makes the condiment, or the seeds can be pressed to make oil and the leaves can be eaten as a salad. It is the seeds I usually use in magical workings (let's face it using the mustard condiment would be pretty messy).

Carry mustard seeds with you or use them in incense blends to keep your mind clear and focused.

Sprinkle mustard seeds around your home for protection.

Eat mustard seeds or use them in medicine pouches to

increase fertility.

Mustard Magical Properties
Clarity, protection, fertility.

Ruling Planet: Mars
Sign: Aries
Element: Fire
Gender: Masculine

Myrrh *(Commiphora myrrha)*
Another natural gum tree resin, this one comes from a thorny tree that has a long history of perfume and incense use.

As with all resins it makes lots of smoke when burnt on charcoal so it works well to protect and purify.

This one also helps you to heal spiritually and emotionally and brings a huge boost of courage with it too.

It has a strong crone energy and is therefore also good for Underworld workings.

I combine myrrh with frankincense a lot as it seems to blend together very well.

Myrrh Magical Properties
Protection, purification, healing, crone, Underworld, courage.

Ruling Planet: Mars, Sun
Sign: Aries, Aquarius
Element: Water
Gender: Feminine

Myrtle *(Myrtus communis)*
This is a flowering evergreen shrub or small tree with fragrant leaves and star-shaped white flowers followed by blue/black berries filled with seeds.

I love the name of this herb, it sounds like an old favourite great aunty.

Aphrodite is often depicted wearing myrtle in her hair and, as it is a feminine energy Venus / moon plant associated with water, it is perfect for love magic.

Use it in protection sachets and incense blends as well as in money workings.

Throw some into the fire to see the name of your true love in the smoke.

Myrtle Magical Properties

Love, protection, money.

Ruling Planet: Venus, Moon
Sign: Taurus
Element: Water
Gender: Feminine

Nettle *(Urtica dioica)*

We can probably all recognise the common stinging nettle as it grows across the world and pretty much on any soil. It normally grows about 2-4 feet high, but in the right conditions I have seen them much taller. The plant has fibrous stems and long-toothed, heart-shaped leaves. The stems and the leaves are covered with coarse, stinging hairs. In summer nettles have bunches of green catkins with male and female flowers on separate plants. Look out for butterflies as several varieties love nettles.

Hans Christian Anderson wrote about stinging nettles in his story *The Wild Swans*, the princess having to weave coats for them out of nettles.

Nettles are also said to mark the place where elves live. Carry nettles with you not only to protect against lightning, but also to draw money to you.

Historically nettles have held the power of protection quite often against demons and witches... eep! They have also been used as anaesthetic and apparently also as a weird kind of rheumatism remedy (apparently the pain of the sting puts the rheumatism pain to shame).

The leaves of the nettle also make a very good green dye.

Nettle is mentioned in an Anglo-Saxon charm recorded in *The Lacnunga*, a 10th century manuscript. The charm is intended to be an antidote to poison and to heal infection. It contains both Pagan and Christian elements and details the Nine Sacred Herbs of Odin.

Nettle it is called, it drives out the hostile one, it casts out poison.
This is the herb that fought against the snake,
It has power against poison; it has power against infection,
It has power against the loathsome foe roving through the land.

Nettle can be used to remove curses and send back hexes. It also works well for exorcism and to protect against negative energies and avert danger.

Use it in amulets and medicine bags to allay fear and ward against ghosts.

Nettles are very good for putting into poppets or witches' bottles to remove curses. Make a magic powder with dried nettles and sprinkle around your property to keep out negative energies. Use nettles in medicine pouches for healing.

Nettle Tea

Ingredients
2 teaspoons dried nettle leaves
½ pint / 1 cup / 250ml of boiling water

Steep for five minutes.

Nettle Magical Properties
Healing, protection, lust, money, exorcism.
Ruling Planet: Mars

Sign: Scorpio, Aries
Element: Fire
Gender: Masculine

Nutmeg *(Myristica fragrans)*

Nutmeg hails from a tall tree with smooth greyish bark that flowers three times a year. It takes nine years before the tree produces its first crop. The nutmeg we are familiar with is the seed, which is covered by an outer shell that we know as mace. They are separated and then dried.

Carry nutmeg with you for good luck and to attract money to you. A whole nutmeg makes an excellent good luck charm.

Sprinkle nutmeg (powdered not lots of whole ones...) around your property to protect against negative energy.

Keep a whole nutmeg under your bed to ensure that fidelity in your relationship stays solid.

Nutmeg is sometimes used in place of High John the Conqueror in spell work.

Nutmeg Magical Properties:

Money, luck, fidelity, protection.
Ruling Planet: Jupiter
Sign: Sagittarius
Element: Fire
Gender: Masculine

Oak *(Quercus alba, Quercus robur, Quercus petraea)*

The oak is ancient, wise and strong.

A sturdy and imposing tree that can grow incredibly tall and live for a thousand years (or so... obviously that's not exact). The leaves are deciduous with catkins in spring and acorns in autumn.

Folklore says: "Oak before ash, in for a splash, ash before oak, in for a soak," referring to the flowers of both trees. If the ash flowers before the oak we usually have a wet spring.

Oak trees were used as meeting places where laws were passed and declarations read out to the public. Oak is sacred to Druids.

It was considered lucky to be married under an oak tree.

The oak leaf symbol is one of strength and used to appear on coins in England (before the lion took over). The fruit from the oak, the acorn is a symbol of strength, power and vitality.

Holly in the form of the Holly King rules the first half of the year up until midsummer then he is replaced by the Oak as the Oak King who rules the second half of the year until the winter solstice.

Hug an oak tree, talk to it, sit with it – allow the oak to help you tap into your inner strength, to bring a new sense of purpose and to allow you to release that which does not serve you.

It is said that King Arthur's round table was made from one solid piece of oak.

Oak has been used to build houses, cathedrals, ships, furniture and barrels, its bark is used for tanning leather. It provides dyes, the acorns are fed to pigs and can also be used as a coffee substitute (the acorns, not the pigs). The galls (oak apples) can be used to make ink, the wood can be used on fires and to make charcoal, the tree provides a favourite home for mistletoe and ivy. It provides shelter for insects, birds, animals and outlaws such as Robin Hood and Charles II. It is a multi-purpose, all use, provider and protector.

If you dream about sitting under an oak tree it means a long life and prosperity.

Burn oak wood in your home to clear out any illness.

Carry an acorn with you to bring good health, youthfulness, fertility and vitality.

Carry oak or an acorn with you to bring good luck.

Oak and acorns are incredibly useful ingredients in magical workings – use them for healing and health pouches; protection, prosperity, fertility and luck amulets and any workings to bring you strength, power and vitality.

Oak hung in your home is said to provide protection from lightning.

Oak Magical Properties

Healing, health, protection, money, fertility, luck, strength, vitality, power.

Ruling Planet: Sun, Jupiter, Mars
Sign: Sagittarius
Element: Fire, Water
Gender: Masculine

Orchid *(Orchidaceae)*

This covers a huge and diverse family of plants with beautiful, exotic and colourful flowers.

Keep an orchid on your altar to remind you of your spirituality.

Use orchid in workings for love and abundance.

Orchid Magical Properties

Spirituality, love, abundance.

Ruling Planet: Venus
Element: Water
Gender: Feminine

Oregano *(Origanum vulgare)*

Oregano is a genus of the mint family and a perennial herb with green scented leaves and purple flowers. It is sometimes called 'wild marjoram' and is a close relative of the culinary herb we know as marjoram.

It is a protective herb, especially against those who would like to interfere in your business, and works well in a floor wash for such a purpose.

Also use oregano in healing spell workings.

Oregano Magical Properties

Ruling Planet: Mars, Venus, Mercury
Sign: Gemini
Element: Air
Gender: Masculine

Pansy *(Viola tricolor)*

A perennial plant, but often grown as annuals, the pansy is a beautifully happy bright and colourful flower coming in all sorts of colours.

Place pansies on your altar to help you focus and find your direction.

Use pansies in all love magical workings; they can help strengthen and deepen love and also attract new love to you.

Use one in rain magic spells. Folklore says that picking a pansy on a sunny day will cause it to rain... but I've also seen the suggestion that picking a pansy at dawn then sprinkling water on it will bring rain.

Pansy represents rebirth so it can be used in workings for that intent.

And you can eat them... which is always a bonus.

Pansy Petal Tea

Ingredients
Tablespoon of rose petals
Teaspoon of pansy petals
One dandelion flower head

Pop the flowers into a tea pot and pour on half a pint of boiling water. Steep for 5-7 minutes then strain and drink. Or you can add the mixture to your floor wash.

Pansy Magical Properties

Love, rain magic, focus, rebirth.

Ruling Planet: Saturn, Venus
Element: Water
Gender: Feminine

Parsley *(Petroselinum crispum, Petrselinum sativum)*

Parsley was eaten to stop rowdiness and becoming drunk... you may have to test it yourself to find out if it works...

Rub parsley on your forehead, temple then heart chakra with the intent of happiness and joy, then burn the parsley to ensure cheerfulness.

Be careful when in the party mood as parsley can also bring on lust and fertility... possibly not always a good combination.

Use parsley in incense blends to uplift and to purify the air. Drop a sprig of parsley into your bath water to cleanse your body from negative energy.

Carry parsley with you for personal protection and apparently that sad sprig of parsley on your plate in a restaurant as garnish is to protect food against contamination.

Parsley seems to have a lot of funereal ties and connections with the dead so makes a good herb to use for Otherworld and spirit work. It was also one of the ingredients often used in flying ointment.

Parsley Magical Properties

Protection, purification, lust, happiness, fertility, spirit work.

Ruling Planet: Mercury
Sign: Gemini, Leo
Element: Air
Gender: Masculine

Passion Flower *(Passiflora)*

Usually a climbing / creeping plant, although some are grown as shrubs, passion flower has the most striking flowers followed by oval fruit.

Its name gives a hint as to one of its magical properties – it works well in love magic, but it also works to calm and bring peace. The passion flower also works well in friendship workings.

Use it in dream pillows to have a restful night's sleep.

Passion Flower Magical Properties

Love, calm, peace, sleep, friendship.

Ruling Planet: Venus
Element: Water
Gender: Feminine

Patchouli *(Pogostemon)*

Although a plant native to tropical climates and not one I can grow in my own garden, I have included it because it is one of my favourites... and it's my book so I can include it if I want. If you can't get hold of the dried herb itself you can use patchouli oil. I have even used crushed up patchouli incense sticks on occasion.

Patchouli is a bushy herb from the mint family with tall stems that have pale pink / white flowers. Patchouli has a strong earthy scent that has been used for centuries in perfume and medicine.

It is an excellent herb for grounding and earth magic and connecting with Mother Earth and her elementals.

Patchouli can be used in all kinds of prosperity and money spells.

It also works very well in protective magic workings.

Patchouli is said to be an aphrodisiac so this herbs works incredibly well in sex magic spells... be warned... it's pretty potent...

Burn it in incense blends to bring balance, peace and calm.

Patchouli Bring You Back Down Incense Blend

This incense blend will ground you and bring your feet back in touch with Mother Earth.

Ingredients
Equal quantities of:
Dried patchouli
Sandalwood
Mugwort

Patchouli Magical Properties

Grounding, earth magic, prosperity, money, protection, sex magic, balance, calm.

Ruling Planet: Saturn
Sign: Virgo
Element: Earth
Gender: Feminine

Pennyroyal *(Mentha / Mentha pulegium)*

This is a small plant from the mint family that takes root easily wherever it lands and flowers in July and August.

Used in the past for initiation rituals and considered a sacred herb of Mother Earth, it works well for initiations (obviously) and any Goddess work.

Keep pennyroyal leaves on you to bring you strength and stamina.

It is a good herb to use in business workings for a successful outcome.

Drink pennyroyal tea or add it to your bathwater to bring calm and peace.

Sprinkle dried pennyroyal around your house to bring in protection.

Pennyroyal Magical Properties

Strength, protection, peace, initiation, Goddess, business.

Ruling Planet: Mars, Venus
Sign: Scorpio, Libra
Element: Fire
Gender: Masculine

Peony *(Paeonia officinalis)*

This hardy perennial shrub produces the most gorgeous flowers.

Plant peonies in your garden to bring good luck, happiness and protection.

Keep peony flowers in your house to dispel negative energy.

Use the dried root in incense blends to bring blessings upon your home.

Peony Magical Properties

Exorcism, protection, luck, happiness, blessings.

Ruling Planet: Sun
Element: Fire
Gender: Masculine

Periwinkle *(Vinca minor)*

An evergreen low-growing, spreading plant, periwinkle has purple / blue five-petal flowers and does have a tendency to take over in gardens if you let it.

The flowers are associated with the Goddess.

Use periwinkle flowers in workings to increase your mental powers.

Add periwinkle to incense blends to bring abundance and love into your life. Also works well to smudge the house to clear negative energy.

Sprinkle periwinkle in your bathwater to help you relax.

Carry some with you for personal protection.

Put periwinkle flowers on the grave of a restless spirit to help them find peace.

Periwinkle Magical Properties

Money, protection, love, lust, mental powers, Goddess, purification, spirit.

Ruling Planet: Venus
Element: Water
Gender: Feminine

Pine *(Pinus)*

Pine is an evergreen conifer tree with thick scaly bark and dark green needles that we often associate with Yule.

The scent of pine is good for bringing us back to ourselves, for centring and focusing.

An excellent herb to use in all kinds of dragon magic.

Pine also brings with it a strong magical protection for your home and also a sense of hospitality and welcome. Keep pine needles in your home to bring in abundance (I would suggest keeping them in a medicine pouch rather than sprinkling them as they are uncomfortable to tread on).

It is also a useful herb to use in truth spells to find out hidden knowledge or secrets.

Use it in incense blends to protect and purify your home or sacred space. I like to add a few drops of pine essential oil to my floor wash.

Use pine cones in fertility magic workings and healing spells.

Pine House Blessing

Light some charcoal in a cauldron or fire-proof container and sprinkle some pine needles on top of the glowing embers. Then pass a pine cone (or cones) through the smoke. Keep the pine cone on your altar or in the hearth of your home to bring blessings and peace to your household.

Pine Magical Properties

Centring, focus, dragon magic, protection, truth, abundance, purification, fertility, healing.

Ruling Planet: Mars, Saturn
Sign: Capricorn
Element: Air, Fire
Gender: Masculine

Plantain *(Plantago spp. Lanceolata, Plantago major, Plantago media)*

A common weed found on footpaths, roadsides and meadows, plantain is a perennial with ribbed leaves and fluffy spikes of flowers on long stalks.

It was one of the nine sacred herbs of the Anglo Saxons, a 'mother of worts' and used for clearing poison and snake bites.

Carry a piece of plantain root in your pocket to protect against snake bites. This also works well as a general protection charm.

Rub plantain on your feet to re-energise.

Hang plantain root over your threshold to ensure that only pleasant people enter your home and place a piece under your bed to keep illness away.

Add a couple of pieces of plantain root to your bathwater to help you relax.

Use in workings for personal strength, protection, healing and to bring you energy and courage.

Protective Plantain Potion

Use one heaped teaspoon dried plantain leaves or one whole fresh leaf to 250ml / one cup of boiling water, steep for 7-10 minutes, then strain. This can be drunk warm for personal protection or tip into your floor wash to bring protection into your home.

Plantain Magical Properties

Strength, protection, healing, energy, courage.

Ruling Planet: Venus
Sign: Capricorn
Element: Earth
Gender: Feminine

Poppy *(Papaver spp)*

An annual plant, the wild poppy has bright red flowers that continue to bloom throughout the summer. The cultivated varieties come in all sorts of colours and I have orange ones in my garden which I like to use in success workings (orange being the colour of success).

Whenever I think of poppies I am reminded of the scene in the *Wizard of Oz* where the poppy field makes them all go to sleep, so it works well in any workings for insomnia and to help with a restful night's sleep. It also represents forgetfulness. The red poppy is also the symbol used to help us remember those brave souls who fell in the world wars.

With the huge amount of seeds a poppy produces, it works well for not only fertility spells but also prosperity and money ones.

Poppy seeds work extremely well to confuse. Sprinkling poppy seeds around your property will confuse any negative or evil spirits; vampires will also be warned off. Apparently vampires are compelled to stop and count the seeds, but I am pretty sure they are far too intelligent to be fooled by this ploy!

I also think that the red poppy represents life, death and rebirth – with the blood red of the petals and the fertility of the seeds.

Adding a pinch of poppy seeds and petals to your bathwater will help you overcome grief.

Poppy Magical Properties

Love, sleep, money, luck, fertility, rebirth, grief.
   Ruling Planet: Moon, Mars, Venus
   Sign: Capricorn
   Element: Water
   Gender: Feminine

Primrose *(Primula vulgaris)*

A beautiful sight at the beginning of spring, primroses grow wild under hedges, on banks and in woods. The long crinkly leaves are downy underneath and put out short stalks covered with yellow, pink or white five-petal flowers. They are a dying species in the wild though, so please I urge you not to pick them; use cultivated ones from your garden for spell work.

Primroses also attract the Fae to your garden and help create a connection to them.

Primrose can be used in workings to help you deal with changes.

Blue and red primroses planted in your garden bring very strong protection; they also bring personal and material growth.

Carry the petals with you for protection and to bring love into your life.

I have also read that they cure madness... but it's never worked for me...

Primrose Magical Properties

Love, protection, faeries, changes, growth.
   Ruling Planet: Venus
   Element: Earth
   Gender: Feminine

Rose *(Rosa spp)*

We must all be familiar with the rose, whether it is as a bush, a climber or in a bunch of flowers. It is a perennial with more varieties and colours than you can shake a stick at. The flowers bloom between May and September and are followed by rosehips. You can also find certain varieties growing in the wild. I have several rose bushes and climbers in my garden and dry all the petals, which is incredibly easy. I sprinkle the petals on a large tray and leave them to dry in the conservatory.

Rose is a good herb to use to represent the mother and also for any workings where mysteries need to be delved into.

Use rose in any workings for love, psychic powers and knowledge. Rose petals are also good for dream work and moon magic.

Roses and the petals have long been associated with love so they work well for any kind of love spells. Use pink roses for friendship, red roses for passion and white roses for peace.

The rose has sharp thorns, so use it in protection workings. It is also a very feminine flower so can be incorporated into any spell or ritual work that requires feminine energy.

Rose also had a connection with death and rebirth, the plant appearing to be dead during the winter months but coming back to life in the spring.

Sprinkle rose petals in your bathwater for a balancing, relaxing and love-filled bath.

Use rose petals in workings for luck and abundance.

Rose petals also work well for casting the circle at handfastings.

Lurve Rose Petal Tea

Ingredients
2 big handfuls of rose petals
2 cups of water
6 lemon balm leaves
2 slices of root ginger
1 stick cinnamon

1 teaspoon honey

Put the rose petals and lemon balm in a pan and cover with the water, simmer on a very low heat for a few minutes until the petals are translucent. Strain and return the liquid to the pan, then add the other ingredients and simmer again for about 10 minutes. Serve warm, best shared with your loved one.

Rose Magical Properties
Love, psychic powers, healing, luck, protection, peace, mysteries, knowledge, dreams, friendship, death and rebirth, abundance.
Ruling Planet: Venus, Moon
Sign: Pisces
Element: Water
Gender: Feminine

Rosemary *(Rosmarinus officinalis)*
A popular herb found in many gardens (apparently introduced to the UK by the Romans), I have several rosemary plants in mine and it grows all year round.

It is an evergreen plant with woody stems, narrow dark green leaves and tiny lilac coloured flowers that bloom twice a year, once in the spring and again in the autumn. The whole plant is aromatic and has a habit of covering you in strongly scented oil whenever you handle the leaves.

Greeks wore rosemary in their hair to help boost the power of memory.

Traditionally rosemary was burnt as incense in houses that were stricken with illness; I like to also use it in my smudge sticks along with lavender and sage.

Grow it, carry it with you or use it in incense blends to bring about protection, healing and purification.

It was often used in bridal bouquets for love and funeral wreaths for remembrance.

Use a long piece of fresh rosemary and bend it into a circle, tie the ends together with ribbon and hang it in your home to bring protection.

Burning rosemary as incense in your home apparently gets rid of unwanted guests or those who have outstayed their welcome.

And yes… it is another one that was used for protection against witches…

I have read that folklore states rosemary will only flourish in the garden where the lady rules the house… (it grows really well in my garden)…

Protection and Purification Rosemary Water

Take a good handful of rosemary (flowers, leaves and stem), place it in a saucepan and cover with cold water. Bring it to the boil, cover and simmer for about 5 minutes. Then transfer it to a jug and allow it to cool, strain and pour into bottles.

This water is excellent to use for sprinkling around your home and property to cleanse and protect, to use for casting a circle in ritual or to cleanse and consecrate ritual tools. It can also be added to bath water or used as a hair rinse.

Rosemary Magical Properties

Protection, love, lust, mental powers, exorcism, purification, healing, sleep.

Ruling Planet: Sun
Sign: Aries
Element: Fire
Gender: Masculine

Rowan *(Sorbus aucuparia)*

Rowan is often found on roadsides and in gardens, woods, heaths and rocky places. It is a smallish tree with grey bark, toothed leaves and white flowers in summer followed by red / orange berries in August and September.

Druids would plant rowan trees near their groves and stone circles for protection against negative energies.

Rowan twigs were carried to ward against sorcery and evil and placed around milk churns to protect against theft.

Rowan has a very strong protective energy, but also one of empowerment. It can help you connect with your inner being, the universe and the web of life all around us.

Bring rowan twigs and berries into your home to use for protection, but also to bring success, love and a stronger spiritual connection.

Thread rowan berries onto red or brown thread to use as a charm for your home or to carry with you to keep you safe on your travels.

Rowan branches make good dowsing rods to help divine for metal. Rowan also makes an excellent healing wand to use intuitively.

Solitary rowan trees are believed to be faerie trees.

Use rowan berries in incense blends for protection, divination, inspiration and to increase your psychic powers.

Tie a handful of rowan berries up in a piece of white cloth and tie it with ribbon. Hang this in the centre of your home (I suggest your kitchen) to keep illness at bay.

Rowan Magical Properties

Psychic powers, power, success, protection, love, spirituality, faeries, divination, healing, inspiration.

Ruling Planet: Sun, Mercury
Sign: Sagittarius
Element: Fire
Gender: Masculine

Rue *(Ruta graveolens)*

Rue is a hardy evergreen shrub with woody stems and yellow flowers during the summer.

Keep rue indoors to create sacred space and burn as incense for protection, purification and balance.

Hang rue above your doorway to ease anxiety and help bring about clarity.

Use it in healing and health workings; it is an incredibly powerful herb to use for protection.

Add rue to your bath to break curses and hexes.

During the Middle Ages it was most definitely considered the herb of witches.

According to my research witches apparently do not like the smell of rue; neither do plague-bearing rats... well that's always good to know...

It is one of the herbs that seem a little confused; it was used by wise women (and men) in a lot of potions, but is another herb that was used in the fight to ward against witches.

Rue Magical Properties

Protection, health, healing, purification, balance, clarity, anxiety, hex breaking.

Ruling Planet: Mars, Sun
Sign: Leo
Element: Fire
Gender: Masculine

Sage (*Salvia officinalis*)

A familiar herb in our gardens, I have the garden / common variety and a pretty purple sage too. It is an evergreen perennial shrub with woody stems and grey leaves (unless you have the purple or variegated varieties) with small lilac coloured flowers.

The white sage (*Salvia apiana*) that is traditionally used for smudging by many American tribes is native to the USA and Mexico. Personally I use the sage that grows in my garden to smudge because it is very similar, I also know that it is free of pesticides and chemicals and I get it for free!

Carry sage with you to ensure wisdom and aid with your intuition.

To cleanse, purify and protect your home, work or ritual space smudge with sage, although I like to add rosemary and lavender into my smudge bundles (but if you have read this book from the start you will know that by now...).

Keep sage on your windowsill to encourage abundance and success.

Write your wish on a sage leaf and place it beneath your pillow; if you dream of your goal then it will come true.

Pick Me Up Sage Tea

Ingredients
1 tablespoon / ½ oz sage leaves (young ones rather than the older, tougher ones)
250ml / 1¼ cups / ½ pint boiling water

Wash the leaves then bruise them slightly with a spoon and pour boiling water on top, leave them to steep for 7-10 minutes, strain and drink to give yourself an energy boost and to lift your spirits. You can also add a teaspoon of honey to make life sweet.

Sage Magical Properties

Protection, wishes, wisdom, purification, stimulating, intuition, abundance, success.

Ruling Planet: Jupiter
Sign: Taurus, Sagittarius
Element: Air
Gender: Masculine

Saint John's Wort *(Hypericum perforatum)*

This is a perennial shrub with light green leaves and bright yellow flowers in summer followed by black seeds.

Plant St John's Wort near your property to bring abundance and protection to your home or hang a piece over your threshold to ward against negative energy.

St John's Wort is used medically to help ease depression, so it works very well in magical workings for happiness. It is a sun herb so brings with it the power to dispel darkness and rules your solar plexus.

Place a piece of St John's Wort under your pillow to dream of your future love.

It was placed in the mouth of an accused witch to help force her to confess to her witchcraft ways, so I think this works well in truth workings. Although how she was expected to confess with a mouthful of herb I really don't know.

And yet it is another herb that historically was used… to ward against witches (sheesh enough already).

Saint John's Wort Magical Properties

Protection, health, strength, love, divination, happiness, abundance, truth.

Ruling Planet: Sun
Sign: Aquarius, Libra
Element: Fire
Gender: Masculine

Sandalwood (White Sandalwood – *Santalum album*) (Red Sandalwood – *Pterocarpus santalinus*)

Red Sandalwood works well in incense blends for meditation and trance work. It doesn't have a lot of scent, but works well in incense blends to keep it burning for longer. Because of its deep red colour it also works well in love magic.

White sandalwood has a very nice scent to it and is often used in funeral rites. It is good to use in purification incense blends.

Use white sandalwood in incense blends to bring desires to fruition and also to increase your psychic abilities.

Sandalwood (Red) Magical Properties

Meditation, love.

Ruling Planet: Venus, Jupiter
Sign: Sagittarius, Virgo
Element: Water
Gender: Feminine

Sandalwood (White) Magical Properties

Death rites, purification, wishes, psychic powers.

Ruling Planet: Moon, Mercury
Sign: Sagittarius, Virgo
Element: Water
Gender: Feminine

Self Heal / All Heal *(Prunella vulgaris)*

This is a perennial herb found on the edges of woodlands and all over grass and scrub land. They are creeping, self-rooting, tough little beggars and can become an annoying weed if left to their own devices. The flowers are purple and white lipped and bloom in the summer months. The leaves and flowers are edible.

Self heal is a good herb to use in medicine pouches and blends to ease stress and bring calm and relaxation in.

Use the flowers either to eat or in magical workings to bring about clarity in a misunderstanding and to make relationships closer.

Use it in meditation blends to help with your spiritual connection.

It was said to be collected by Druids and used in magic cleansings to clear a person from being 'faery struck'.

It works well in floor washes to purify and cleanse.

Self Heal Magical Properties

Releasing, cleansing, spirituality, stress, calming, clarity, protection.

Ruling Planet: Venus
Element: Water
Gender: Feminine

Scullcap *(Scutellaria)*

Scutellaria is a genus of annual or perennial flowering plants from the mint family. The flowers have upper and lower lips and resemble miniature medieval helmets.

Use it in spell working for faithfulness and prosperity spells.

This is a good herb to use in workings to pep you up after you have been spiritually or psychically attacked or after any exorcism work.

Add it to magical workings to relieve stress and bring peace and calm to your life.

Scullcap Magical Properties

Faithfulness, restoring, prosperity, stress, peace.
Ruling Planet: Saturn
Sign: Virgo
Element: Water
Gender: Feminine

Sea Holly *(Eryngium spp)*

Sea holly is an annual and perennial plant with spiny leaves that carries pale blue or white flowers; although it is called 'holly' it is not related to the holly family.

Carry some with you to bring luck and safety on a journey.

Use it in incense blends and workings to bring about peace after an argument.

Add it to love magic spells.

Sea Holly Magical Properties

Travel, peace, love.
Ruling Planet: Venus

Element: Water
Gender: Feminine

Snapdragon *(Antirrhinum majus)*

Grown as annuals, snapdragons have pretty coloured flowers that resemble the mouth and head of a dragon.

Legend has it that antirrhinums were planted on the graves of successful dragon slayers (boooooo).

The dragon connection does make these little flowers brilliant to use in any kind of dragon magic and also good for working with elementals.

Add it to your incense blends or pop some of the flowers on your altar to assist you with your divination skills.

This is another plant that has traditionally been planted around your property to protect against witchcraft (sigh) so turn that around and use it to our advantage – work with these flowers for protection. They also work well to break hexes.

To protect against deceit and find out the truth carry snapdragon with you.

Keep snapdragon seeds under your pillow to prevent nightmares and give you a good night's sleep.

Snapdragon Magical Properties

Dragon magic, divination, elementals, protection, hexes, truth, sleep, nightmares.

Ruling Planet: Mars
Sign: Gemini
Element: Fire
Gender: Masculine

Solomon's Seal *(Polygonatum officinale)*

A flowering plant that grows from rhizomes, it is the root that is generally used in magical workings. Graceful arching stems appear in the spring with oval leaves and dangling white bell-shaped flowers throughout spring and early summer.

There are lots of stories about where this plant got its name from such as the root resembling royal seals, the cut root looking like Hebrew characters and the scar from the stem dying back on the root looking like the Star of David.

The root and leaves of this plant carry the magic of Solomon so work especially well in wisdom and knowledge workings.

Carry some with you for protection and success or use it in exorcism rites. Place a piece of the root in the four corners of your house to create a protective boundary.

The root also works well to aid in calling upon the elementals.

Use the leaves in incense blends to cleanse, protect and purify your home or sacred space.

Solomon's Seal Magical Properties

Wisdom, knowledge, protection, exorcism, success, elementals, purification.

Ruling Planet: Saturn
Sign: Capricorn
Element: Water
Gender: Feminine

Sorrel (Wood) (*Oxalis acetosella*)

A perennial and an annual, this plant grows across the world and has many species within the genus. Most have three leaflets to the green leaves and white, pink, red or yellow five-petal flowers.

The leaves of wood sorrel are carried to ward against heart disease so this herb works well not only in healing spells, but also in workings dealing with affairs of the heart.

Wood sorrel has incredibly strong earth energies so is excellent to use for grounding.

Sorrel Magical Properties

Healing, health, love, grounding.

Ruling Planet: Venus
Sign: Capricorn, Taurus
Element: Earth
Gender: Feminine

Star Anise *(Illicium verum)*

An ancient herb, the star shape seeds of star anise come from an evergreen shrub and the seedpods are picked just before the fruit ripens and are dried in the sun. The star shape of the seed lends itself to all sorts of magical correspondences and representations. They have a delicious aniseed aroma and taste.

Place star anise in the corner of each room in your home to bring luck. Keep a whole star anise on your altar to help keep a spiritual connection. Place a star anise beneath your pillow to induce prophetic dreams and also to help you sleep.

Burn star anise as an incense to purify and protect your home and also to help increase your psychic powers or wear one in an amulet or pouch to provide psychic protection and keep away evil.

Make a sachet of star anise and bay to pop into your bath water to purify and cleanse your aura and energies.

This is also a good herb to use in new moon rituals and spell work.

Star Anise Magical Properties

Luck, psychic powers, purification, protection, dreams, spirituality, sleep.

Ruling Planet: Jupiter
Sign: Cancer or Leo
Element: Air
Gender: Masculine

Sunflower *(Helianthus annuus)*

An annual that can grow incredibly tall, the stem is slightly hairy with large leaves and the flower itself is a large flat disk of seeds surrounded by bright yellow petals. The flower head always turns to face the sun, which makes them good to use in loyalty workings.

Aztec priestesses would wear sunflowers and they would be placed in Aztec temples.

Obviously this flower carries with it a huge punch of masculine sun energy (the name is a bit of a giveaway).

If you need to know the truth about a situation sleep with a sunflower under your bed (presumably just the flower head otherwise it wouldn't fit…), this would work with sunflower seeds too.

Bring sunflower into your home to promote integrity.

Growing sunflowers in your garden will bring you good luck and protection.

Eat sunflower seeds for fertility and add them to fertility workings (they also taste quite yummy).

Also use sunflower seeds in workings to make wishes come true.

Sunflower is an incredibly happy, bouncy, cheerful kind of a flower so I find it works well in happiness spells (the seeds or the petals). You can also add a handful of sunflower petals to your bathwater to make you feel happy and content.

I've also seen 'secret hideaways' created by planting sunflowers in a circle in your garden. Once they grow to a decent height you can sit inside. It would make a lovely ritual circle.

Sunflower Magical Properties

Wishes, fertility, truth, integrity, luck, protection, loyalty, happiness.

Ruling Planet: Sun
Sign: Leo
Element: Fire
Gender: Masculine

Sweetgrass *(Hierochloe odorata)*

This is a hardy perennial grass with a sweet slightly vanilla scent when burnt that grows on the edges of marshes and wet meadowlands.

Sweetgrass (sometimes called holy grass) is often sold plaited or tied into a smudge stick. Burn it to cleanse and purify any area. When made into a plait the strands represent mind, body and spirit.

Burn as incense and allow your wishes to be carried away on the smoke. The scent of the smoke is also very uplifting.

Hang a braid of sweetgrass above your doorway for protection.

Sweetgrass Magical Properties

Cleansing, purification, wishes, protection, uplifting.

Ruling Planet: Venus

Element: Air, Water

Sweetpea *(Lathyrus odoratus)*

Climbing annuals (although there is a perennial variety too), these plants like the sunshine and give off the most amazing scent. Although they are of the pea family please note that they are poisonous.

Sweetpea not only brings a beautiful scent, it also brings in peace, love, joy and new friendships.

Carry sweetpea with you to ensure you always tell the truth.

Wearing the flowers will bring you physical and spiritual strength.

They are a spiritual flower and can be used in workings to help you connect with spirit and deepen your psychic abilities.

Sweet pea works in medicine pouches to protect children. Also use in sleep workings to bring on a peaceful and restful night's sleep.

Sweetpea Magical Properties

Courage, strength, friendship, peace, happiness, truth, spirituality, psychic abilities, protection, sleep.

Ruling Planet: Venus, Moon, Mercury

Element: Water

Gender: Feminine

Tansy *(Tanacetum vulgare)*

A hardy perennial plant with tall stems topped with green leaves and bright yellow, tansy flowers from July to September. It can be found on river banks, grass verges and waste ground.

This herb was used in a lot of cooking... tansy pudding and tansy cakes being traditional... must be why I like it.

Traditionally used in funeral rites, this herb symbolises death and rebirth and in guiding the spirit onto the Otherworld.

The flowers last a long time so represent longevity; carry with you to increase your life span (apparently).

Carry tansy in your pocket to remind you of your birthright and who you are.

It is a good herb to use when working with the Dark Goddesses.

Bring some tansy into your house to clear out any illnesses and improve health. This herb can also be used to 'draw out' any illness and must then be burnt (the herb... not the person) to remove the disease or virus.

Carry some with you to ensure a safe journey when travelling.

Use it in cleansing and protection workings and incense blends.

Tansy Magical Properties

Health, longevity, rebirth, cleansing, protection, travel.

Ruling Planet: Venus

Sign: Gemini

Element: Water

Gender: Feminine

Thistle *(Carduus spp)*

Thistles have lots of dark purple flowers on tall stems, all of which along with the leaves are covered in prickles and sharp edges.

Keep thistle flowers on your altar to strengthen your connection with spirit.

Put thistle down under your doorstep to stop thieves from entering the house.

Keep thistles in the room where someone is poorly, they will help with the healing process.

Use in protection and healing spell workings and in poppets for hex breaking.

Thistle Magical Properties

Protection, healing, exorcism, hex breaking, spirit.

Ruling Planet: Mars, Jupiter
Element: Fire
Gender: Masculine

Thyme *(Thymus vulgaris, Thymus serpyllum)*

A low growing woody herb with small green leaves and tiny lilac-coloured flowers that bloom throughout the summer, this herb smells and tastes delicious. Wild thyme can be found growing in woods, fields, and commons and on heath lands.

It is an excellent herb to use in any healing workings (and in culinary use for healing too).

Burn it in incense blends or carry with you for good health. Also use it in incense blends to purify and cleanse your home and bring love and peace in.

Thyme will increase your willpower and give you courage.

Making (and drinking) thyme tea will help you release the past; you can also add the tea mix to your bath water.

Sleep with thyme under your pillow to ensure a good night's sleep and mix thyme with lavender to make a brilliant sleep pillow.

Romans would wash their faces in thyme water to enhance their attractiveness and carry it with them to ward off venomous creatures.

Thyme Magical Properties

Healing, health, peace, psychic powers, love, purification, courage, releasing, sleep, beauty.

Ruling Planet: Venus
Sign: Gemini, Taurus, Libra
Element: Water
Gender: Feminine

Tobacco *(Nicotiana spp)*

This is an annual plant with long roots and wrinkled leaves.

Burn tobacco leaves to cleanse and purify an area (although this does sound a bit weird as stale tobacco smoke is not nice, but it does cleanse negative energies).

Mix ground tobacco leaves with some cornmeal or salt and sprinkle around your property to bring in protection.

If you are working with earth energies in your magic, leave an offering of tobacco afterwards. Sprinkle some into water if you are intending to travel across it, to ensure a safe journey.

Caution: This plant is poisonous, but then you knew that already.

Tobacco Magical Properties.

Purification, travel, protection.

Ruling Planet: Mars
Element: Fire
Gender: Masculine

Tulip *(Tulipa spp)*

These are beautiful spring flowers that grow from bulbs and come in every colour.

Place a tulip on your altar or beside your bed to attract or keep a lover.

Tulips help you to expand your ability to love and release any fears connected with it.

Plant tulips in your garden to bring peace to your home and abundance and prosperity to your life.

Keep tulip seeds or petals in your purse or wallet to ensure you always have money.

Tulip Magical Properties

Love, peace, protection, prosperity.

Ruling Planet: Venus
Element: Earth
Gender: Feminine

Turmeric *(Curcuma longa)*

Turmeric is a perennial plant with long tuberous roots; it is this part that is used to make the spice we are familiar with.

Dissolve turmeric and salt in water to make a blessing and purifying liquid to sprinkle around your home, work place or ritual area. Be careful as turmeric does stain, unless you want everything to turn bright yellow...

Put a piece of turmeric root above your threshold to protect your home.

Use turmeric in incense blends to purify and bring peace to your house.

Turmeric Magical Properties

Purification, protection, peace.

Ruling Planet: Mars
Element: Fire, Air

Gender: Feminine

Valerian (*Valeriana officinalis*)

Valerian is a perennial plant that grows in ditches and near rivers with dark green leaves and tall flower stems topped with clusters of pink flowers during July and August. It is the root that is usually used in magical workings.

Hang valerian root above your doorway to protect your home and to bring about a sense of peace. It can also be used in workings to ease stress and calm your nerves.

Wear valerian root in an amulet to attract love to you.

Valerian root can be placed in pillows to induce sleep (grind it to a powder first otherwise it would be incredibly uncomfortable).

It works well in incense blends to invoke animal spirits and to purify and cleanse an area.

Valerian Magical Properties

Protection, purification, love, sleep, peace, animal spirit, stress.

Ruling Planet: Venus, Jupiter
Sign: Virgo
Element: Water, Earth
Gender: Feminine

Vervain (*Verbena officinalis*)

A perennial with spikes of small white or lilac coloured flowers in late summer, vervain can be found growing on verges and grassland. Harvest at the end of flowering; when dry remove the larger stems and crush the rest into small pieces.

Traditionally Druids used vervain for divination, consecrating and cleansing of ritual spaces. A potion was made that included vervain and represented the Awen from Cerridwen's cauldron, which inspired poetry, song and bardic tales. Drinking vervain tea will connect you with the Underworld, inspire you, aid in divination and psychic work and help you to connect with spirit. It is also a good herb to help with shape shifting.

Picking vervain used to be accompanied by a prayer, which I like the idea of – with any herb, flower or plant that I pick I always ask first and tell the plant what I will be using it for.

Use vervain to purify and cleanse your home, work place and ritual space (King Solomon was said to have used vervain for that purpose). Use vervain in water to cleanse and consecrate rituals tools or in your bathwater before a ritual.

Burn vervain in incense blends to bring about purification and protection. Roman soldiers would carry vervain with them to protect them in battle. Romans also sprinkled it around their homes to keep evil spirits away.

Medicinally vervain is a good herb for stress relief and bringing calm so it works very well in workings to bring about peace and relaxation. It is also considered an aphrodisiac, so add it to your love workings… but be careful on the amounts used…

Carry vervain with you to bring about protection and attract love to you.

Bury a piece of vervain on your property to help the flow of money coming into your life.

Chill-Out Chai

Use one heaped teaspoon of dried vervain to a mugful of boiling water, steep for 5-7 minutes, strain, then drink.

Vervain Magical Properties

Protection, love, purification, peace, sleep, healing, money, inspiration, shape shifting.

Ruling Planet: Venus
Sign: Gemini
Element: Earth
Gender: Feminine

Violet *(Viola odorata)*

A spring flowering plant, the leaves of the violet are heart shaped with pretty purple or white flowers that bees love.

White violets represent innocence and humility. Blue violets stand for loyalty, consistency and steadfastness.

Carry a violet with you to ease your heart from unrequited love (ahhhhhh).

Keep violets in your home or plant them in your garden to bring about peace, healing and protection.

Use violets in all kinds of love and lust workings and don't be fooled by their size; for a small flower they pack a powerful punch of magic.

Violets also remind us to be true to ourselves and to be committed to what we do.

Violets are also associated with death and rebirth (the myth of Attis and the story of Persephone).

Violet Magical Properties

Love, lust, peace, healing, protection, commitment, death and rebirth.

Ruling Planet: Venus
Sign: Cancer, Libra
Element: Water
Gender: Feminine

Walnut *(Juglans regia)*

This is a tall, sturdy tree with a large canopy. Small flowers are followed by the walnut fruit, which ripen in September.

Work with the energy of walnut to help increase your mental clarity and help with decision making.

Sleep with a walnut under your bed to increase fertility.

Use walnut shells as 'holders'; write your wishes on small pieces of paper and pop them inside a walnut shell, bury or burn them to set the intent of your wishes.

Walnut Magical Properties

Wishes, mental powers, clarity, fertility.

Ruling Planet: Sun
Element: Fire
Gender: Masculine

Willow *(Salix alba, Salix fragilis)*

A tall deciduous tree found on riverbanks and hedgerows, the leaves and flowers of the willow appear in April / May. This tree always seems to be jam-packed full of emotions for me, whether it is because it has the element of water or because it is ruled by the moon... or maybe both.

The wood of the willow tree is incredibly versatile and can be used for making wicker baskets, clogs, cricket bats and charcoal, which was even used at one time to make gunpowder.

The young flexible branches of the willow can be plaited together to make small besoms for cleansing and sweeping ritual areas or made into witches' ladders for spell work. You can also use the bendy branches for knot magic. Stand under the moon and as you state your intent out loud, then tie a knot in the willow branch, sealing your intent.

Write your wish on a piece of willow bark then burn or bury it to manifest your desire.

Carry willow with you or burn it in incense blends to bring about inspiration and to enhance your intuition.

To bring love to you sleep with a piece of willow under your bed.

Mix with sandalwood in incense blends to use during the waning moon for releasing and letting go.

Caution: do not ingest willow if you are allergic to aspirin or whilst breastfeeding.

Willow Love Wreath

Using three flexible willow branches, plait them together then tie them into a circle to make a wreath. You can do this by using pink or red ribbon. You could even plait some of the ribbon in with the willow as you go.

Hang the wreath above your bed to keep your love harmonious or hang it in the centre of your home to bring love into the house.

Moon Goddess Incense Blend

Ingredients
Equal parts of each:
Willow bark
Rose petals
Frankincense
Sage
Pine

Willow Magical Properties

Love, protection, healing, cleansing, wishes, release, inspiration, intuition.

Ruling Planet: Moon
Sign: Pisces
Element: Water
Gender: Feminine

Witch Hazel (*Hamamelis virginiana*)

Witch hazel is a shrub / small tree that grows with twisty, turny, crooked branches with smooth grey bark. Yellow flowers appear in autumn after the leaves have fallen, followed by a black nut filled with seeds.

It is a good protective wood to use, but also excellent to make divining rods from. The rods will help you find underground sources of water, but also any lost items.

To overcome grief and find inner emotional balance carry

witch hazel leaves.

Witch Hazel Magical Properties

Protection, divining, balance, grief.

Ruling Planet: Sun, Saturn
Sign: Capricorn
Element: Fire
Gender: Masculine

Woodruff *(Asperula odorata, Galium odoratum)*

A widespread and commonly found herb in woods and on banks, woodruff is a perennial that spreads, but the roots can be easily damaged when harvesting so be careful when picking. It has green leaves with tiny white flowers that appear in spring and early summer and have a nice scent.

Burn woodruff in incense blends to purify, cleanse and bring in protection. It will also herald the energies of balance and empowerment.

Use in workings for justice and to attract money to you.

Sprinkle woodruff around your home and property to bring about positive changes.

The woodruff flowers are also sacred to the Goddess.

Sweet Woodruff Success Tipple

Ingredients
Small handful of fresh woodruff flowers
3 strawberries
3 raspberries
3 cups of apple juice
2 slices of orange
1 slice of apple
2 teaspoons vanilla sugar (sugar that has been kept with a vanilla pod in, or add a couple of drops of vanilla extract)

Rinse the woodruff and the fruit then mix all the ingredients together. This is lovely served chilled over ice or works well as a drink in ritual.

Woodruff Magical Properties

Protection, money, balance, justice.

Ruling Planet: Mars
Element: Fire
Gender: Masculine

Wormwood *(Artemisia absinthium)*

Wormwood is a perennial plant grown for its silvery green pretty leaves and also used as an ingredient in the alcoholic drink absinthe, which I have tasted and only just lived to tell the tale...

This herb is used in magic for vengeance, revenge and attacking... on your own karma be it...

It is very protective so use in magic workings or carry it with you.

Use it in dream workings, journeying and divination spells.

Burn it as an incense to increase your psychic abilities.

Wormwood Magical Properties

Vengeance, attack magic, protection, divination, dreams, meditation, psychic powers.

Ruling Planet: Mars, Moon
Sign: Cancer, Scorpio
Element: Fire
Gender: Masculine

Yarrow *(Achillea millefolium)*

A perennial plant with feathery dark green leaves and heads of white or occasionally pink flowers during summer and early autumn, yarrow can be found on roadsides and in meadows.

Achilles used yarrow as a field dressing for the wounds of his soldiers during the Trojan War; he obviously didn't have enough left to use on his heel...

The herb was often referred to as the Devil's plaything and indeed during the 17th century a woman was tried as a witch for using yarrow in her spells, but let's not get into the 'there is no devil in witchcraft' thing!

Yarrow was used by the Druids for weather prediction and young ladies would use it to show a vision of who their true love might be. Dried yarrow heads were originally used in the divination method of I-Ching.

Carry yarrow with you to allay fears and bring you personal courage.

Keep yarrow under your pillow to enhance prophetic dreams.

Drink yarrow tea or burn as incense to increase your psychic powers.

Bring yarrow into your home or burn it as an incense blend to invite love, happiness and peace.

Scatter yarrow around your property or wear in an amulet to keep you protected.

Yarrow Magical Properties

Psychic powers, love, courage, exorcism, dreams, peace, happiness, divination, protection.

Ruling Planet: Venus
Element: Water
Gender: Feminine

Yew *(Taxus baccata)*

Yew is a tall evergreen tree with a thick brown trunk. The leaves are dark green and narrow with red berries that follow on from the flowers.

The yew tree has a history of being associated with death and rebirth and can often be found in graveyards. The yew tree is a reminder that although death occurs, it opens up a door for rebirth and renewal. The tree is very sacred to Druids and yew tree groves were planted by ancient burial mounds and sacred sites.

It is a winter solstice tree standing between the two worlds – the tree of death and the tree of life. It was said the yew tree marked the entrance to the Underworld. Working with yew can open you up to transformation and connect you with your ancestors and the knowledge that they have for you. It can also help with astral travel.

Use in workings where the past needs to be released so that forward motion can be achieved.

I would not advise burning yew in any way (on fires or in incense) as most parts of the tree are poisonous. Stick with the wood, the roots and dried leaves / berries for magical pouches and spell work only. The wood makes lovely wands and runes; I have a beautiful wand made from the root of a yew tree.

The yew tree also corresponds to the crone aspect of the Goddess.

Yew Magical Properties

Death and rebirth, transformation, astral travel, ancient knowledge, knowledge.

Ruling Planet: Saturn, Mercury
Element: Water, Earth
Gender: Feminine

Herb Code Names

A lot of fairy stories and folk tales talk of witches adding ingredients to their cauldrons such as 'eye of newt' and 'wing of bat'. There is some truth to this, but in actual fact they weren't using animal parts (well not always...) they were in fact folk names for plants. Some of these folk code names date back to 40-90AD. Here are some of the more well known ones:

Adder's Tongue: Dogstooth Violet, Plantain
Ass's Foot: Coltsfoot
Bat's Wing: Holly leaf
Bat's Wool: Moss
Bear's Foot: Lady's Mantle
Bird's Eye: Germander, Speedwell
Blood: Elder sap or another tree sap
Blood from a Head: Lupine
Blood from a Shoulder: Bear's Breeches
Blood of a Goose: Mulberry tree's sap
Blood of a Hamadryas Baboon: Blood of a spotted gecko
Blood of a Snake: Hematite
Blood of an Eye: Tamarisk gall
Blood of Ares: Purslane
Blood of Hephaistos: Wormwood
Blood of Hestia: Chamomile
Bloody Fingers: Foxglove
Blue Jay: Bay Laurel
Bone of an Ibis: Buckthorn
Brains: Cherry tree gum (this phrase usually designates any fruit tree gum)
Bull's Blood or Seed of Horus: Horehound
Bull's Foot: Coltsfoot
Bull's Semen: Eggs of the Blister Beetle

Calf's Snout: Snapdragon
Capon's Tail: Valerian.
Cat: Catnip
Cat's Foot: Canada Snake Root and/or Ground Ivy
Clot: Great Mullein
Corpse Candles: Mullein
Cuddy's Lungs: Great Mullein
Crocodile Dung: Ethiopian Earth
Crow Foot: Cranesbill, Wild Geranium, Buttercup
Devil's Dung: Asafoetida
Dog: Couch Grass
Dog's Mouth: Snapdragon
Dog's Tongue: Hounds Tongue
Dove's Foot: Wild Geranium
Dragon's Blood: Resin of Draco Palm
Dragon's Scales: Bistort leaves
Eagle: Wild Garlic or Fenugreek
Ear of an Ass: Comfrey
Ears of a Goat: St. John's Wort
Englishman's Foot: Common Plantain
Eye of Christ: Germander, Speedwell
Eye of the Day: Common Daisy
Eye of the Star: Horehound
Eyes: Inner part of a blossom, Aster, Daisy, Eyebright
Fat from a Head: Spurge
Fingers: Cinquefoil
Five Fingers: Cinquefoil
Foot: Leaf
Frog: Cinquefoil
Frog's Foot: Bulbous Buttercup
From the Belly: Earth-Apple
From the Foot: Houseleek
From the Loins: Chamomile
Goat's Foot: Ash Weed

God's Hair: Hart's Tongue Fern
Gosling Wing: Goosegrass
Graveyard Dust: Mullein
Great Ox-eye: Ox-Eye Daisy
Guts: The roots and stalk of a plant
Hair: Dried stringy herbs, ripe male Fern
Hair of a Hamadryas Baboon: Dill seed
Hair of Venus: Maidenhair Fern
Hare's Beard: Great Mullein
Hawk: Hawkweed
Hawk's Heart: Wormwood seed or Wormwood crown
Head: Flower of a plant
Heart: Walnut; bud, seed, or nut
Hind's Tongue: Hart's Tongue Fern
Horse Hoof: Coltsfoot
Horse Tongue: Hart's Tongue Fern
Jacob's Staff: Great Mullein
Jupiter's Staff: Great Mullein
King's Crown: Black Haw
Kronos' Blood: Cedar
Lamb: Lettuce
Lamb's Ears: Betony
Leg: Leaf
Lion's Hair: Tongue of a Turnip (i.e., the leaves of the taproot])
Lion's Tooth: Dandelion aka Priest's Crown
Lion Semen: Human semen
Man's Bile: Turnip sap
Nightingale: Hops
Paw: Leaf
Physician's Bone: Sandstone
Pig's Snout: Dandelion
Pig's Tail: Leopard's Bane
Priest's Crown: Dandelion
Privates: Seed

Ram's Head: American Valerian
Rat: Valerian
Red Cockscomb: Amaranth
Seed of Horus: Horehound
Semen of Ammon: Houseleek
Semen of Ares: Clover
Semen of Helios: White Hellebore
Semen of Hephaistos: Fleabane
Semen of Herakles: Mustard-Rocket
Semen of Hermes: Dill
Shepherd's Heart: Shepherd's Purse
Skin of Man: Fern
Skull: Skullcap Mushroom
Snake: Bistort
Snake's Ball of Thread: Soapstone
Snake's Head: Leech
Sparrow's Tongue: Knotweed
Swine's Snout: Dandelion leaves
Tail: Stem
Tears of a Hamadryas Baboon: Dill juice
Teeth: Pine cones
Titan's Blood: Wild Lettuce
Toad: Toadflax, Sage
Toe: Leaf
Tongue: Petal
Unicorn's Horn: False Unicorn Root, True Unicorn Root
Urine: Dandelion
Weasel: Rue
Weasel Snout: Yellow Dead Nettles / Yellow Archangel
White Man's Foot: Common Plantain
Wing: Leaf
Wolf Claw: Club Moss
Wolf Foot: Bugle Weed
Wolf's Milk: Euphorbia

Woodpecker: Peony
Worms: Thin roots

Victorian Flower Language

Although flowers have had 'meanings' for centuries, it was the Victorians that really jumped on the band wagon with this idea; a particular flower or the scent of one on a handkerchief could send a very important message to a suitor. It was a whole 'secret' language devised to send messages or convey meanings in the form of flowers. The list is huge and varied but the following will give you some idea.

Apple Blossom: Good fortune
Aster: Love
Azalea: Passion, take care
Bachelor's Buttons: Celibacy
Balm: Sympathy
Begonia: Beware
Bittersweet: Truth
Bluebell: Gratitude, humility
Broom: Humility
Buttercup: Riches, childlike
Camellia (pink): Longing
Camellia (white): Adoration, perfect
Camellia (red): Passion
Carnation (pink): Never forget you
Carnation (red): My heart longs for you
Carnation (white): Innocence, pure love
Carnation (yellow): Disappointment
Celandine: Joy
Chickweed: Holding on to you
Chrysanthemum: Abundance
Chrysanthemum (white): Truth
Chrysanthemum (red): Love
Cornflower: Refinement

Cowslip: Healing, youth, grace
Crocus: Cheer, gladness
Cyclamen: Goodbye
Daffodil: Respect, unrequited love
Dahlia: Dignity, elegance, forever yours
Daisy: Innocence, loyalty, pure, beauty
Dandelion: Faithful, happiness
Delphinium: Fun
Dill: Lust
Edelweiss: Courage
Elderflower: Zeal
Euphorbia: Persistence
Forget Me Not: True Love, memories
Forsythia: Anticipation
Foxglove: Youth
Freesia: Trust, innocence
Fuchsia: Love
Gardenia: Secret love, purity
Geranium: Friendship
Gerbera: Innocence
Gladioli: Generosity
Goldenrod: Be cautious, encouragement
Harebell: Humility, grief
Heather: Admiration, wishes
Heliotrope: Devotion
Hibiscus: Consumed by love
Holly: Defence, forgotten
Hollyhock: Fruitfulness
Honesty: Sincerity
Honeysuckle: Love
Hyacinth: Consistency, sorry
Hydrangea: Understanding
Iris: Faith, promise, hope
Ivy: Affection

Jasmine: Sensuality, grace
Larkspur: Open heart
Lavender: Love, devotion
Lilac: Beauty, pride, emotions
Lily (white): Purity
Lily (yellow): False, gratitude
Lily of the Valley: Sweetness, happiness
Magnolia: Nobility
Mallow: Beauty, sweetness
Marigold: Love, affection, sorrow
Marjoram: Happiness
Mint: Virtue
Mistletoe: Affection, kisses
Morning Glory: Affection
Motherwort: Secret love
Mugwort: Tranquillity
Mullein: Good nature
Myrtle: Love, joy
Nasturtium: Conquest
Oak: Bravery
Orchid: Love, beauty
Pansy: You are in my thoughts
Parsley: Knowledge
Peach Blossom: I am captivated
Peony: Shame, happy marriage, compassion
Periwinkle: Memories
Petunia: I am soothed by you
Poppy (red): Pleasure
Poppy (white): Consolation
Poppy (yellow): Success
Primrose: I can't live without you
Rhododendron: Danger
Rose (pink): Happiness, secret love, indecision
Rose (red): Love

Rose (white): Innocence, silence
Rose (yellow): Joy, jealousy
Rosemary: Remembrance
Sage: Wisdom, respect
Snapdragon: Gracious, strength
Snowdrop: Hope, consolation
Sunflower: Adoration
Sweetpea: Thank you but goodbye
Tulip: Perfect
Tulip (red): Believe me
Tulip (yellow): Your smile is sunshine
Valerian: Accommodating
Verbena: Sensibility
Vervain: Enchantment
Violet: Modesty, affection, virtue
Wormwood: Do not be discouraged
Yarrow: Heartache cure

Intent Correspondence List

This lists the herbs by their intent, but once again this is only a list taken from traditional and historic uses and my own experiences. When it comes down to it, it is your magic, so go with your own intuition.

Abundance
Bergamot, Buttercup, Camellia, Clove, Cornflower (Batchelor's Buttons), Cumin, Dandelion, Echinacea, Frankincense, Grass, Heliotrope, Horseradish, Hyacinth, Ivy, Orchid, Pine, Rose, Sage, Saint John's Wort

Attack Magic
Wormwood

Ancient Wisdom
Buttercup, Yew

Astral Travel
Belladona, Morning Glory, Mugwort, Yew

Anxiety
Cramp Bark, Lemon Balm, Rue

Balance
Alyssum, Chamomile, Dill, Elm, Holly, Honeysuckle, Patchouli, Rue, Witch Hazel, Woodruff

Baneful spells
Belladonna

Banishing
Bergamot (orange)

Beauty
Thyme

Beginnings (New)
Birch, Crocus

Binding
Cleavers, Cypress, Ivy, Knotweed

Blessings
African Violet, Crocus, Fenugreek, Goldenrod, Peony

Bringing Together
Comfrey

Business
Pennyroyal

Calming
Aloe, Alyssum, Benzoin, Chamomile, Cowslip, Lungwort, Mint,
Passion Flower, Patchouli, Self Heal

Cat Magic
Catnip

Centring
Mullein, Pine

Changes
Cinnamon, Primrose

Clarity
Bergamot, Betony, Cardamom, Clove, Columbine (Aquilegia), Dill, Horehound, Juniper, Knotweed, Lavender, Mustard, Rue, Self Heal, Walnut

Cleansing
Agrimony, Alexanders, Burdock, Dock, Geranium, Ginger, Gourd, Heather, Horsetail, Lily of the Valley, Lungwort, Mint, Mugwort, Self Heal, Sweetgrass, Tansy, Willow

Commitment
Cleavers, Violet

Confidence
Benzoin, Black Pepper, Fennel

Consecration
Aster, Ginger, Mace

Courage
Angelica, Birch, Borage, Carnation, Catnip, Columbine (Aquilegia), Daisy, Fennel, Myrrh, Plantain, Sweetpea, Thyme, Yarrow

Creativity
Bay, Beech

Crone Magic
Belladonna, Echinacea, Myrrh

Death Rites
Sandalwood (white)

Depression (Anti)
Betony, Lemon Balm

Divination
Angelica, Beech, Blackthorn, Buttercup, Cinquefoil, Dandelion, Eucalyptus, Foxglove, Hazel, Iris, Lily of the Valley, Morning Glory, Rowan, Saint John's Wort, Snapdragon, Witch Hazel, Wormwood, Yarrow

Dragon Magic
Delphinium, Dragon's Blood, Pine, Snapdragon

Dreams
Ash, Bergamot, Bracken, Catnip, Chamomile, Fidelity, Cinquefoil, Daisy, Datura, Eucalyptus, Heather, Heliotrope, Holly, Iris, Jasmine, Marigold, Mistletoe, Mugwort, Rose, Star Anise, Wormwood, Yarrow

Earth Magic
Magnolia, Patchouli

Elementals
Snapdragon, Solomon's Seal

Emotions
Alexanders

Energy
Coltsfoot, Elm, Plantain

Escape
Celandine

Exorcism

Angelica, Basil, Birch, Black Pepper, Blackthorn, Clove, Clover, Cumin, Daffodil, Elder, Garlic, Heliotrope, Horehound, Horseradish, Juniper, Lilac, Mint, Nettle, Peony, Rosemary, Solomon's Seal, Thistle, Yarrow

Faeries

Columbine (Aquilegia), Cornflower (Batchelor's Buttons), Delphinium, Elder, Evening Primrose, Fern, Foxglove, Hawthorn, Heather, Lavender, Lily of the Valley, Primrose, Rowan

Faithful

Dogwood, Scullcap

Feminine Energy

Datura, Evening Primrose, Mugwort

Fertility

Birch, Bracken, Catnip, Chickweed, Cornflower (Batchelor's Buttons), Cyclamen, Daffodil, Dock, Fennel, Geranium, Hawthorn, Hazel, Horsetail, Mistletoe, Mustard, Oak, Parsley, Pine, Poppy, Sunflower, Walnut

Fidelity

Caraway, Chickweed, Clover, Cumin, Ivy, Magnolia, Nutmeg

Focus

Cinnamon, Frankincense, Pansy, Pine

Forgiveness

Hawthorn, Heliotrope

Friendship
Bergamot, Heather, Passion Flower, Rose, Sweetpea

Goddess Magic
Aster, Cedar, Lily, Pennyroyal, Periwinkle

Gossip (Stopping and Preventing)
Black Pepper, Clove, Foxglove, Marigold

Grief (Coping With)
Cypress, Marjoram, Poppy, Witch Hazel

Grounding
Patchouli, Sorrel

Growth
Primrose

Happiness
African Violet, Agrimony, Basil, Borage, Catnip, Celandine, Crocus, Cyclamen, Daisy, Dragon's Blood, Hawthorn, Hyacinth, Lavender, Lily of the Valley, Marigold, Marjoram, Meadowsweet, Parsley, Peony, Saint John's Wort, Sunflower, Sweetpea, Yarrow

Harmony
Dulse

Healing / Health
Anemone, Angelica, Ash, Bay, Blackthorn, Bluebell, Bracken, Burdock, Calamus, Caraway, Carnation, Cinnamon, Coltsfoot, Comfrey, Coriander, Cowslip, Cramp Bark, Dock, Echinacea, Elder, Eucalyptus, Fennel, Feverfew, Flax, Garlic, Hazel, Horehound, Hyssop, Ivy, Juniper, Knotweed, Lemon Balm, Lungwort, Marjoram, Mint, Mistletoe, Mugwort, Myrrh, Nettle,

Oak, Pine, Plantain, Rose, Rosemary, Rowan, Rue, Saint John's Wort, Sorrel, Tansy, Thistle, Thyme, Vervain, Violet, Willow

Healing (Spiritual)
Agrimony, Cypress

Hex Breaking
Angelica, Cinquefoil, Comfrey, Datura, Elder, Horseradish, Lily, Rue, Snapdragon, Thistle

Hope
Crocus, Hawthorn

Hunting (Not Just Prey, Also Jobs / Relationships)
Evening Primrose

Initiation
Caraway, Fennel, Pennyroyal

Inspiration
Hazel, Rowan, Vervain, Willow

Integrity
Sunflower

Intoxication (Anti)
Betony

Intuition
Alexanders, Ash, Elder, Sage, Willow

Invisibility
Fern

Jealousy
Black Pepper, Columbine (Aquilegia), Dill, Garlic

Justice
Juniper, Woodruff

Knot Magic
Flax, Grass

Knowledge
Dill, Goldenrod, Rose, Solomon's Seal, Yew

Legal Matters
Celandine

Longevity
Chrysanthemum, Horsetail, Tansy

Lost (Items)
Aster

Love
Agrimony, Ash, Aster, Basil, Benzoin, Betony, Birch, Bleeding
Heart, Caraway, Cardamom, Catnip, Chamomile, Chestnut,
Chickweed, Cinnamon, Cinquefoil, Cleavers, Clove, Clover,
Coltsfoot, Columbine (Aquilegia), Copal, Coriander, Cornflower
(Batchelor's Buttons), Crocus, Cumin, Cyclamen, Daffodil, Daisy,
Dandelion, Dill, Dittany of Crete, Dock, Dragon's Blood, Dulse,
Elm, Fern, Frankincense, Geranium, Ginger, Hawthorn, Hazel,
Heather, Horehound, Hyacinth, Iris, Ivy, Jasmine, Juniper, Lady's
Mantle, Lavender, Lemon Balm, Lilac, Lobelia, Lovage, Mallow,
Mandrake, Marjoram, Meadowsweet, Mistletoe, Myrtle, Orchid,
Pansy, Passion Flower, Periwinkle, Poppy, Primrose, Rose,
Rosemary, Rowan, Saint John's Wort, Sandalwood (red), Sea

Holly, Sorrel, Thyme, Tulip, Valerian, Vervain, Violet, Willow, Yarrow

Loyalty
Dogwood, Sunflower

Luck
Agrimony, Aloe, Angelica, Beech, Broom, Calamus, Clover, Daffodil, Elm, Hazel, Heather, Holly, Horseradish, Marigold, Nutmeg, Oak, Peony, Poppy, Rose, Star Anise, Sunflower

Lust
Benzoin, Caraway, Cinnamon, Cumin, Cyclamen, Daisy, Dill, Dragon's Blood, Dulse, Honeysuckle, Jasmine, Nettle, Parsley, Periwinkle, Rosemary, Violet

Magic
Cinquefoil, Dill, Lily of the Valley

Maiden Magic
Alyssum

Marriage
Marjoram

Meditation
Bergamot, Cramp Bark, Fenugreek, Goldenrod, Honeysuckle, Horseradish, Jasmine, Lilac, Sandalwood (red), Wormwood

Memory
Betony, Caraway, Honeysuckle, Lemon Balm

Mental Powers
Periwinkle, Rosemary, Walnut

Moon Magic
Aloe, Chickweed, Eucalyptus, Evening Primrose, Iris

Money
Basil, Bergamot (orange), Bladder wrack, Calamus, Cedar, Chamomile, Clove, Clover, Comfrey, Dill, Dock, Fenugreek, Flax, Ginger, Goldenrod, Gorse, Honesty, Jasmine, Mint, Myrtle, Nettle, Nutmeg, Oak, Patchouli, Periwinkle, Poppy, Vervain, Woodruff

Monsters
Honesty

Mysteries
Rose

Negativity (Dispels / Repels)
Agrimony, Ash, Black Pepper, Clove, Coriander

Nightmares (Preventing)
Betony, Cyclamen, Fenugreek, Hyacinth, Mullein, Snapdragon

Passion
Cardamom

Peace
Alyssum, Basil, Borage, Coltsfoot, Coriander, Cowslip, Cumin, Dulse, Feverfew, Horehound, Hyacinth, Lavender, Meadowsweet, Passion Flower, Pennyroyal, Rose, Scullcap, Sea Holly, Sweetpea, Thyme, Tulip, Turmeric, Valerian, Vervain, Violet, Yarrow

Power
Bay, Cinnamon, Dragon's Blood, Echinacea, Ginger, Oak, Rowan

Prosperity

Ash, Basil, Benzoin, Camellia, Fenugreek, Hazel, Honeysuckle, Mandrake, Patchouli, Scullcap, Tulip

Protection

African Violet, Agrimony, Aloe, Alyssum, Anemone, Angelica, Ash, Aster, Basil, Bay, Benzoin, Betony, Birch, Black Pepper, Blackthorn, Bladder wrack, Bluebell, Borage, Bracken, Broom, Burdock, Buttercup, Calamus, Caraway, Cardamom, Carnation, Cedar, Celandine, Chickweed, Chrysanthemum, Cinnamon, Cinquefoil, Clove, Clover, Comfrey, Copal, Coriander, Cornflower (Batchelor's Buttons), Cramp Bark, Cumin, Cyclamen, Cypress, Daffodil, Daisy, Datura, Delphinium, Dill, Dittany of Crete, Dogwood, Dragon's Blood, Dulse, Elder, Fennel, Fern, Feverfew, Flax, Foxglove, Garlic, Geranium, Ginger, Gorse, Gourd, Grass, Hawthorn, Hazel, Heather, Heliotrope, Holly, Honeysuckle, Horehound, Hyssop, Ivy, Juniper, Lavender, Lilac, Lily, Lobelia, Lovage, Mallow, Mandrake, Marigold, Marjoram, Mint, Mistletoe, Mugwort, Mullein, Mustard, Myrrh, Myrtle, Nettle, Nutmeg, Oak, Parsley, Patchouli, Pennyroyal, Peony, Periwinkle, Pine, Plantain, Primrose, Rose, Rosemary, Rowan, Rue, Sage, Saint John's Wort, Self Heal, Snapdragon, Solomon's Seal, Star Anise, Sunflower, Sweetgrass, Sweetpea, Tansy, Thistle, Tobacco, Tulip, Turmeric, Valerian, Vervain, Violet, Willow, Witch Hazel, Woodruff, Wormwood, Yarrow

Psychic Abilities / Powers

Aloe, Bay, Bladder wrack, Borage, Buttercup, Cinnamon, Cornflower (Batchelor's Buttons), Dandelion, Elm, Fenugreek, Grass, Honeysuckle, Juniper, Mace, Marigold, Morning Glory, Mugwort, Rose, Rowan, Sandalwood (white), Star Anise, Sweetpea, Thyme, Wormwood, Yarrow

Purification

Bay, Bergamot (orange), Betony, Birch, Broom, Cedar, Chamomile, Copal, Dock, Elder, Eucalyptus, Fennel, Feverfew, Frankincense, Hawthorn, Horseradish, Hyssop, Iris, Juniper, Lobelia, Mace, Myrrh, Parsley, Periwinkle, Pine, Rosemary, Rue, Sage, Sandalwood (white), Solomon's Seal, Star Anise, Sweetgrass, Thyme, Tobacco, Turmeric, Valerian, Vervain

Re-Birth

Cramp Bark, Elder, Pansy, Poppy, Rose, Tansy, Violet, Yew

Relationships

Cleavers

Relaxing

Chamomile, Cramp Bark, Frankincense

Releasing

Alexanders, Birch, Carnation, Celandine, Coriander, Cypress, Lungwort, Self Heal, Thyme, Willow

Restoring

Scullcap

Sea Magic

Alexanders, Ash, Bladder wrack

Self-Esteem

Cyclamen

Sex Magic

Patchouli

Shape Shifting
Bluebell, Heather, Vervain

Sleep
Agrimony, Bergamot, Chamomile, Hyacinth, Lavender, Passion Flower, Poppy, Rosemary, Snapdragon, Star Anise, Sweetpea, Thyme, Valerian, Vervain

Social
Geranium

Snakes
Horsetail

Spell Reversal
Agrimony

Spirit Work
Dittany of Crete, Fern, Heather, Parsley, Periwinkle, Thistle, Valerian (animal spirit work)

Spirituality
African violet, Alyssum, Bay, Beech, Camellia, Chrysanthemum, Cinnamon, Frankincense, Heliotrope, Orchid, Rowan, Self Heal, Star Anise, Sweetpea

Stimulating
Sage

Stolen items
Juniper

Strength
Bay, Black Pepper, Carnation, Daisy, Garlic, Horseradish,

Horsetail, Lavender, Mugwort, Oak, Pennyroyal, Plantain, Saint John's Wort, Sweetpea

Stress Relief
Betony, Clove, Cramp Bark, Self Heal, Scullcap, Valerian

Success
Beech, Bergamot (orange), Cinnamon, Clover, Cumin, Ginger, Holly, Lemon Balm, Lily of the Valley, Rowan, Sage, Solomon's Seal

Sun Magic
Bergamot (orange), Eucalyptus

Tenacity
Cleavers

Tension
Cramp Bark

Theft (Anti)
Cumin

Tranquillity
Coltsfoot

Transformation
Yew

Travel
Comfrey, Sea Holly, Tansy, Tobacco

Treasure
Cowslip

Truth
Bluebell, Clove, Honesty, Pine, Saint John's Wort, Snapdragon, Sunflower, Sweetpea

Trust
Dogwood

Underworld
Fern, Myrrh

Uplifting
Bergamot (orange), Cardamom, Sweetgrass

Vengeance
Wormwood

Visions
Coltsfoot, Crocus, Dittany of Crete

Visitors (Anti)
Cowslip

Vitality
Oak

Wealth
Basil, Coriander

Weather Magic
Bladder wrack, Broom, Heather, Lobelia, Pansy

Wisdom
Hazel, Iris, Sage, Solomon's Seal

Wishes

Beech, Dandelion, Hazel, Sage, Sandalwood (white), Sunflower, Sweetgrass, Walnut, Willow

Witchcraft

Lily

Worries

Knotweed

Youth

Cowslip

Element Correspondence List

Earth

Beech, Cornflower (Batchelor's Buttons), Cramp Bark, Cypress, Dogwood, Echinacea, Grass, Honesty, Honeysuckle, Horsetail, Knotweed, Lungwort, Magnolia, Mugwort, Patchouli, Plantain, Primrose, Sorrel, Tulip, Valerian, Vervain, Yew

Air

Agrimony, Alyssum, Beech, Benzoin, Bergamot, Bergamot (orange), Birch, Borage, Bracken, Broom, Caraway, Clover, Columbine (Aquilegia), Dandelion, Dock, Eucalyptus, Fenugreek, Fern, Goldenrod, Hazel, Horehound, Lavender, Lemon Verbena, Lily of the Valley, Mace, Marjoram, Meadowsweet, Mint, Mistletoe, Morning Glory, Parsley, Pine, Sage, Star Anise, Sweetgrass, Turmeric

Fire

Anemone, Angelica, Ash, Basil, Bay, Betony, Black Pepper, Blackthorn, Buttercup, Carnation, Cedar, Celandine, Chestnut, Chrysanthemum, Cinnamon, Cinquefoil, Cleavers, Clove, Copal, Coriander, Cumin, Dill, Dittany, Dragon's Blood, Fennel, Flax, Frankincense, Garlic, Ginger, Gorse, Hawthorn, Heliotrope, Holly, Horseradish, Hyssop, Juniper, Lovage, Mandrake, Marigold, Mullein, Mustard, Nettle, Nutmeg, Oak, Pennyroyal, Peony, Pine, Rosemary, Rowan, Rue, St John's Wort, Snapdragon, Sunflower, Thistle, Tobacco, Turmeric, Walnut, Witch Hazel, Woodruff, Wormwood

Water

African Violet, Alexanders, Aloe, Ash, Aster, Belladonna, Birch, Bladder wrack, Bleeding Heart, Bluebell, Burdock, Calamus, Camellia, Cardamom, Catnip, Chamomile, Chickweed, Coltsfoot,

Columbine (Aquilegia), Comfrey, Cornflower (Batchelor's Buttons), Cowslip, Crocus, Cyclamen, Daffodil, Daisy, Delphinium, Dittany of Crete, Dulse, Elder, Eucalyptus, Evening Primrose, Feverfew, Foxglove, Geranium, Gourd, Heather, Hyacinth, Iris, Ivy, Jasmine, Lady's Mantle, Lemon Balm, Lilac, Lily, Lobelia, Mallow, Myrrh, Myrtle, Oak, Orchid, Pansy, Passion Flower, Periwinkle, Poppy, Rose, Sandalwood (Red), Sandalwood (White), Self Heal, Scullcap, Sea Holly, Solomon's Seal, Sweetgrass, Sweetpea, Tansy, Thyme, Valerian, Violet, Willow, Yarrow, Yew

Gender Correspondence List

Feminine

African Violet, Aloe, Alyssum, Aster, Beech, Belladonna, Bergamot, Birch, Bladder wrack, Bleeding Heart, Bluebell, Burdock, Calamus, Camellia, Cardamom, Catnip, Chickweed, Cleavers, Coltsfoot, Columbine (Aquilegia), Comfrey, Cornflower (Batchelor's Buttons), Cowslip, Cramp Bark, Crocus, Cyclamen, Cypress, Daffodil, Daisy, Datura, Delphinium, Dittany of Crete, Dittany, Dulse, Echinacea, Elder, Elm, Eucalyptus, Evening Primrose, Foxglove, Geranium, Goldenrod, Heather, Honesty, Horsetail, Hyacinth, Iris, Ivy, Jasmine, Knotweed, Lady's Mantle, Lemon Balm, Lilac, Lily, Lobelia, Magnolia, Mallow, Mugwort, Mullein, Myrrh, Myrtle, Orchid, Pansy, Passion Flower, Patchouli, Periwinkle, Plantain, Poppy, Primrose, Rose, Sandalwood (red), Sandalwood (white), Self Heal, Scullcap, Sea Holly, Solomon's Seal, Sorrel, Sweetpea, Tansy, Thyme, Tulip, Turmeric, Valerian, Vervain, Violet, Willow, Yarrow, Yew

Masculine

Agrimony, Alexanders, Anemone, Angelica, Ash, Basil, Bay, Benzoin, Bergamot (orange), Betony, Black Pepper, Blackthorn, Borage, Bracken, Broom, Buttercup, Caraway, Carnation, Cedar, Celandine, Chamomile, Chestnut, Chrysanthemum, Cinnamon, Cinquefoil, Clove, Clover, Copal, Coriander, Cumin, Dandelion, Dill, Dock, Dogwood, Dragon's Blood, Fennel, Fenugreek, Fern, Feverfew, Flax, Frankincense, Garlic, Ginger, Gorse, Gourd, Hawthorn, Hazel, Heliotrope, Holly, Honeysuckle, Horehound, Horseradish, Hyssop, Juniper, Lavender, Lemon Verbena, Lily of the Valley, Lovage, Lungwort, Mace, Mandrake, Marigold, Marjoram, Meadowsweet, Mint, Mistletoe, Morning Glory, Mustard, Nettle, Nutmeg, Oak, Parsley, Pennyroyal, Peony, Pine,

Rosemary, Rowan, Rue, Sage, St John's Wort, Snapdragon, Star Anise, Sunflower, Thistle, Tobacco, Walnut, Witch Hazel, Woodruff, Wormwood

Planet Correspondence List

Jupiter

Agrimony, Betony, Birch, Borage, Cedar, Chestnut, Cinquefoil, Clove, Copal, Dandelion, Dock, Honeysuckle, Hyssop, Juniper, Meadowsweet, Nutmeg, Oak, Sage, Sandalwood (red), Star Anise, Thistle, Valerian

Mars

Anemone, Basil, Belladonna, Black Pepper, Blackthorn, Broom, Cardamom, Coriander, Cumin, Dragon's Blood, Echinacea, Garlic, Ginger, Gorse, Hawthorn, Holly, Horseradish, Mustard, Myrrh, Nettle, Oak, Pennyroyal, Pine, Poppy, Rue, Snapdragon, Thistle, Tobacco, Turmeric, Woodruff, Wormwood

Mercury

Bergamot (orange), Bluebell, Bracken, Caraway, Cinquefoil, Clover, Dill, Elm, Fennel, Fenugreek, Fern, Flax, Horehound, Lavender, Lemon Verbena, Lily of the Valley, Lungwort, Mace, Mandrake, Marjoram, Mint, Mullein, Parsley, Rowan, Sandalwood (white), Sweetpea, Yew

Moon

Aloe, Birch, Bladder wrack, Calamus, Camellia, Chickweed, Dittany, Dulse, Eucalyptus, Evening Primrose, Gourd, Honesty, Hyssop, Iris, Ivy, Jasmine, Juniper, Lemon Balm, Lily, Mallow, Mugwort, Myrtle, Poppy, Rose, Sandalwood (white), Sweetpea, Willow, Wormwood

Neptune

Ash, Lobelia, Morning Glory

Saturn

Aloe, Beech, Belladonna, Blackthorn, Cleavers, Comfrey, Cornflower (Batchelor's Buttons), Cypress, Datura, Elm, Foxglove, Holly, Horsetail, Ivy, Knotweed, Lobelia, Mullein, Pansy, Patchouli, Pine, Scullcap, Solomon's Seal, Witch Hazel, Yew

Sun

Angelica, Ash, Bay, Benzoin, Bergamot (orange), Buttercup, Calamus, Carnation, Cedar, Celandine, Chamomile, Chrysanthemum, Cinnamon, Copal, Eucalyptus, Frankincense, Hazel, Heliotrope, Juniper, Lovage, Mace, Marigold, Mistletoe, Morning Glory, Myrrh, Oak, Peony, Rosemary, Rowan, Rue, St John's Wort, Sunflower, Walnut, Witch Hazel

Venus

African Violet, Angelica, Aster, Benzoin, Birch, Bleeding Heart, Burdock, Cardamom, Catnip, Coltsfoot, Columbine (Aquilegia), Cornflower (Batchelor's Buttons), Cowslip, Crocus, Cyclamen, Daffodil, Daisy, Datura, Delphinium, Dittany of Crete, Echinacea, Elder, Feverfew, Flax, Foxglove, Geranium, Goldenrod, Hawthorn, Heather, Hyacinth, Iris, Jasmine, Lady's Mantle, Lemon Balm, Lilac, Lily, Magnolia, Mallow, Mint, Mugwort, Myrtle, Orchid, Pansy, Passion Flower, Pennyroyal, Periwinkle, Plantain, Poppy, Primrose, Rose, Sandalwood (red), Self Heal, Sea Holly, Sorrel, Sweetgrass, Sweetpea, Tansy, Thyme, Tulip, Valerian, Vervain, Violet, Yarrow

Sign Correspondence List

Aries
Bay, Cinnamon, Clove, Clover, Coriander, Cowslip, Dragon's Blood, Feverfew, Frankincense, Garlic, Ginger, Horseradish, Juniper, Marjoram, Mustard, Myrrh, Nettle, Rosemary

Aquarius
Bergamot (orange), Borage, Crocus, Cypress, Elder, Fennel, Frankincense, Iris, Mint, Mullein, Myrrh, St John's Wort

Cancer
Agrimony, Angelica, Caraway, Catnip, Daisy, Dill, Honeysuckle, Hyssop, Jasmine, Lemon Balm, Mandrake, Mint, Mugwort, Star Anise, Violet, Wormwood

Capricorn
Benzoin, Comfrey, Copal, Buttercup, Marjoram, Pine, Plantain, Poppy, Solomon's Seal, Sorrel, Witch Hazel

Gemini
Angelica, Bergamot, Betony, Caraway, Cinquefoil, Dill, Honeysuckle, Lavender, Meadowsweet, Mint, Parsley, Snapdragon, Tansy, Thyme, Vervain

Leo
Angelica, Bay, Borage, Burdock, Chamomile, Daffodil, Dill, Fennel, Frankincense, Heliotrope, Lavender, Marigold, Mint, Mistletoe, Parsley, Rue, Star Anise, Sunflower

Libra
Angelica, Aster, Bergamot, Burdock, Catnip, Elder, Feverfew, Pennyroyal, St. John's Wort, Thyme, Violet

Pisces

Bladder wrack, Dulse, Fern, Geranium, Lemon Verbena, Lily of the Valley, Lungwort, Meadowsweet, Rose, Willow

Sagittarius

Agrimony, Aloe, Beech, Betony, Birch, Cedar, Elder, Feverfew, Hawthorn, Mace, Nutmeg, Oak, Rowan, Sage, Sandalwood (red), Sandalwood (white)

Scorpio

Basil, Blackthorn, Cowslip, Horehound, Ivy, Lady's Mantle, Lily, Nettle, Pennyroyal, Wormwood

Taurus

Cinquefoil, Coltsfoot, Daisy, Dandelion, Fern, Iris, Lovage, Lungwort, Mandrake, Mint, Myrtle, Sage, Sorrel, Thyme

Virgo

Bergamot (orange), Fennel, Mandrake, Patchouli, Sandalwood (red), Sandalwood (white), Scullcap, Valerian

Sabbat Correspondence List

Each sabbat also has herb associations. Again, this is just a short list to get you started; go with what works for you.

Samhain
Bay, Broom, Catnip, Garlic, Heather, Mandrake, Mugwort, Mullein, Nettle, Oak, Passion Flower, Patchouli, Pine, Rosemary, Rue, Sage, Sunflower, Wormwood

Yule / Winter Solstice
Birch, Cedar, Cinnamon, Cloves, Elder, Frankincense, Hazel, Holly, Ivy, Mistletoe, Myrrh, Nutmeg, Oak, Pine, Rose, Sandalwood

Imbolc
Ash, Basil, Benzoin, Celandine, Chamomile, Coriander, Dragon's Blood, Frankincense, Garlic, Heather, Myrrh, Rosemary, Sage, Witch Hazel, Vervain, Violet

Ostara / Spring Equinox
Broom, Celandine, Cinquefoil, Crocus, Daffodil, Dogwood, Elder, Honeysuckle, Jasmine, Lavender, Lemon Balm, Lily of the Valley, Lilac, Lovage, Marjoram, Meadowsweet, Oak, Rose, Tansy, Thyme, Tulip, Violet, Vervain, Willow

Beltane
Ash, Broom, Cinquefoil, Coriander, Daffodil, Dogwood, Dragon's Blood, Elder, Fern, Flax, Frankincense, Hawthorn, Marigold, Marjoram, Meadowsweet, Nettle, Self Heal, Rose, Rue, Snapdragon, Thistle, Woodruff

Litha / Summer Solstice

Basil, Chamomile, Cinquefoil, Elder, Fennel, Fern, Feverfew, Hazel, Heather, Honeysuckle, Hyssop, Iris, Lavender, Meadowsweet, Mistletoe, Mugwort, Oak, Pansy, Parsley, Pine, Rosemary, Rowan, Rue, Sage, Saint John's Wort, Sunflower, Thyme, Vervain

Lughnasadh / Lammas

Aloe, Basil, Blackthorn, Clover, Comfrey, Elder, Frankincense, Garlic, Goldenrod, Heather, Heliotrope, Ivy, Marigold, Meadowsweet, Mint, Mugwort, Myrtle, Peony, Poppy, Rose, Sunflower, Vervain, Yarrow

Mabon / Autumn Equinox

Benzoin, Chamomile, Fern, Frankincense, Marigold, Mistletoe, Myrrh, Oak, Passionflower, Rosemary, Rue, Sage, Sunflower, Sweetgrass, Thistle, Walnut, Yarrow

Dark Magic Herbs

These are herb suggestions for what might be considered 'darker' aspects of magic... but on your own head be it... With magic comes responsibility although we are all entitled to defend and protect ourselves.

Return
To send negative intent and energy back to its source: Agrimony, Ginger, Mullein, Nettle, Rue, Thistle

Deflect
Deflection against ill intent: Blackthorn, Elder, Ginger, Mullein, Nettle, Pennyroyal, Pepper, Rue, Willow, Star Anise

Return and Seal
Return negative intent and energy back to the sender and keep it there: Blackthorn, Elder, Rue, Willow

Cursing
I don't mean rude words (although you might like to add them), I mean sending curses and hexes: Cypress, Dragon's Blood, Rowan, Wormwood, Yarrow

Flowers by Month

Months of the year and birthdays as well often have flowers associated with them; here is a basic list to work from.

January: Carnation, Snowdrop
February: Violet, Iris, Primrose
March: Daffodil
April: Daisy, Sweetpea
May: Hawthorn, Lily, Lily of the Valley
June: Honeysuckle, Rose
July: Delphinium/Larkspur
August: Gladioli, Poppy
September: Aster, Forget-Me-Not, Morning Glory
October: Marigold
November: Chrysanthemum
December: Holly, Poinsettia

Deities

Some herbs and plants are often associated with particular deities (or vice versa). As always (are you bored with me saying this yet?) go with your instinct and intuition for this – I am not going to list all the deities (it would need a separate book on its own), but if you want to use herbs to honour a specific deity look at the characteristics, personality and traits of that deity and then match them to a herb intent. So for instance Aphrodite is a Goddess of love so take a look at the 'love intent' list of herbs and see which ones *you* feel will work best – you get the gist.

A Happy Herbal Ending...

Herb magic is powerful and many of the plants are multi-purpose. You don't need to use *all* of the herbs for each intent otherwise you would be carrying a wheelbarrow full of herb parts around with you and you wouldn't be able to get into your house because of all the herb charms. Stick with a few ingredients in each spell working, less is most definitely more and I think keeping it simple keeps the intent clear.

At the end of the day it is *your* magic that makes it all work.

MOON

BOOKS

Moon Books invites you to begin or deepen your encounter with Paganism, in all its rich, creative, flourishing forms.